Casting for Gold

CASTING FOR GOLD

John Bailey

The Crowood Press

First published in 1991 by
The Crowood Press Ltd
Ramsbury, Marlborough
Wiltshire SN8 2HR

British Library in Cataloguing Publication Data

Bailey, John
Casting for gold.
1. Angling
I. Title
799.12092

ISBN 1 85223 453 9

This book is dedicated to the memories of Denis Mitchell and Morris
Metha

Acknowledgements
Photographs by John Bailey

Thanks for help, ideas and additional photography go to Roger Miller, Joy
Hurst, Gordon Heath, John Hett, John McDonald, Norrie, John Conway,
Pete Rogers, Gord Burton, Alan Smith, Fred Buller, Margaret Broadley,
Pete Smith, Paul Harris, Des Elliott, Alwyne Wheeler, Chris Currie, Colin
Dyson, Linda Mitchell, Peter Nicholson, George, and John and Joe.

Typeset by Taurus Graphics
Printed in Great Britain by
Butler & Tanner Ltd, Frome

Contents

Introduction

Casting for Gold follows hard on the heels of *In Wild Waters*, a book written over the years of 1987 and 1988 and which was well received when it was published in 1989. This new book has been compiled over 1989 and 1990 and extends the scene without, I hope, losing sight of the original principles; a stroll on the wilder side of British specialist angling. Now the stage is extended to Ireland, south-east Europe and Asia but always the search is for fish that have a British history and a British feel to them.

Even the Asian mahseer owes its fame to the days of the British Raj; the Anglo-Indians who fished for them between 1880 and 1947 are as worthy angling heroes as Hugh Tempest Sheringham, Francis Francis or Richard Walker himself. Wandering on the banks of the upper Ganges, I could console myself with the thought that anglers who had learnt their art on Scottish burns and English streams had stood in my exact footsteps a century before me. The mahseer itself looked in most lights simply like a massive wild carp . . . and fought like one too! The point I want to make is that exotica are not my thing at all. Billy-a-bong boneheads, Samoan angelfish and all the rest, are not for me. If a fish did not make its impact on me during the 1950s, where I spent my childhood in the north-west of England, then it is probably too late now. A true fisherman cannot fabricate a passion. The desire for a fish has to be real to be of any use and my obsession with carp, barbel, pike, ferox trout and even mahseer date back to the days when I cried myself to sleep for a week over the death of the Busby Babes in the air crash that wiped out that heavenly Manchester United Team.

Since I wrote *In Wild Waters* my life has changed course rather dramatically in that teaching and I have given each other up. This has allowed me the time, if not exactly the cash, to travel and fish more extensively than in the past.

I have always held strongly the view that there are two major ways to approach fishing. The first of these is to concentrate on a water close to home that you can fish at any time of almost every day. This way you quickly build up a picture of the lake and its fish, and understand in exact detail the aquatic environment. Travelling-time is very short and fishing periods are therefore greatly extended. This type of local fishing breeds an intimacy and oneness with nature that is admirable and instructive. It is the fishing of childhood when a bicycle is all that young anglers need to get to their own paradise.

Many anglers live out their fishing lives in this way. Indeed, I have half a dozen waters in England and in Scotland to which I return again and again, always with a new love, always with fresh ideas and always ready to be taught new lessons whenever I go. Anglers, more than most people, should be in tune with the earth around them and to many sensitive people the whole idea of travel by plane or car is abhorrent. A person touching the soil, however, is able to derive from it all manner of energies. Indeed Werner Herzog, the famous film-maker, believing this, once walked from Munich to Paris through ice and snow to spirit death away from the door of a close friend.

Certainly modern travel to far-flung waters can make you wish with all your heart for the local pond. Never did I want my feet on the ground more than recently on the boat to Ireland. Holyhead was hardly behind us when the effect of a force nine was felt. Grey faces all round! I found myself toilet bound within ten minutes and met outside a queue a cricket pitch long. No good. I decided on sleep. This was hard but better, I found, than sitting upright. Just to make things worse the boat was making slow progress against the rising gale. This was a nightmare that seemingly would last forever. I was told that I was the worst on the ship. 'Praise' like this sparked me into a show of defiance and I wandered out on to a storm-thrashed deck where Irish priests ministered and where desperate screaming could be heard from windward . . . an oriental being sick found it being blown back into his own face!

Car travel I have found to be little better. Even Scotland, for example, is well over 500 miles from my door and a journey littered with caravans and, even worse, the inevitable roadworks. Now I generally travel overnight but there have been hazards. One particular journey illustrates this well. It was May in 1988. I was still playing football then and had been involved in a cup game. We all drank from the piece of silverware and I left East Anglia just after midnight. By 3 a.m. I was well up the A1. Finding myself to be running out of petrol I stopped at an all-night service station. I filled up the car and walked over to the locked kiosk to pay. As I drew out my cheque-book, two men appeared from a van hidden in a dimly lit corner of the forecourt. As I wrote out the amount and signed they took their place in this queue of three behind me. The face of the cashier was strained and I sensed trouble. I turned, putting the cheque-book back into my pocket, and one of the men said, 'We'll have that'. I did not really pause to think. Normally I am yellow to the core, but perhaps I was tired or angered still by a kick I had received in the game the night before. Anyway, I threw a punch. The first man crumpled and I ran to the car which mercifully started first time. After only a few miles, however, I realized that my wrist was sprained and swelling. I drove on until 6 a.m. when the pain grew intense. By now I was thoroughly shaken by the incident and tired out. I was driving more and more slowly and only just made the Dick Down Hotel for breakfast. Immediately I was out on the loch but made a string of errors. Finally in the early afternoon I gave up and collapsed on a sun-facing island. I had an early dinner and was in bed at 8.30 p.m. I slept for exactly twelve and a half hours and never moved. The bedside lamp was still on, a glass of port was untouched, my book was still open on page one when I awoke.

Nor are arrivals always easy. I remember trying to find a cottage in Yugoslavia, around 1 a.m., after a nightmare of a journey over what seemed a thousand miles of pot-holes and behind every sheep in the Balkans. I was saved by a town drunk who had crashed his car into a ditch and was still able to give approximate information by weak German, even weaker English and voluble Serbian! I followed his craggy finger to find a light and a farmer's wife tending to a goat in the kitchen. She was able to direct me precisely. The cottage was rat-infested and smelt desperately but it was still a roof over my head in a distant place.

Despite all these hazards I still feel the urge to travel and to fish. There is a glorious unpredictability now about life. Concentration on basic needs is unusual in the modern world of guaranteed comforts, and most modern, 'First World' worries seem to fall away. Bills, domestic chores, a clean car and a weed-free garden are no longer important. Finding a bed or some food becomes the prime task of the night. Time takes on a new pace. Days seem to become longer and the weeks are less compressed. There is a new awareness of life as it unfolds before you. Nothing now can be taken for granted and a sudden weather change can produce a wind to blow your head off or a sunburst that will cook you red in an hour. There is a real joy of new waters to look forward to, an unexpected big fish or giants lost at the net. There is a promise of snapping tackle and splintering rod butts! You endure without food for days and suddenly you are treated to a feast.

Perhaps, in a far-flung country, somebody gives a surprise party for you and you are guaranteed a hangover from unknown liquor. Perhaps a rare bird will be spotted or an old friend re-met. You wake up at dawn to a day where anything might happen.

Travelling brings a richness to your angling full of new challenges, new solutions and even new dangers. You are fishing now on an ever expanding horizon. Travelling also brings a richness both to the eye and to the soul. You fish in wonderfully fresh landscapes and catch unmarked fish. You meet fascinating people with intriguing customs in the most unusual places. You make fine friendships that stay firm through thick and thin, and reveal nothing but the positive side of human nature. Above all, to travel is to follow dreams. Myth and reality rarely go hand in hand and disappointments are legion. But there can be times when such a massive fish takes you that you wonder whether you are really awake or still dreaming. . .

Of course, any angler preparing to travel for his sport must consider carefully the practicalities before setting out. When travelling by car, Five Star travel insurance is essential. A vehicle breakdown far from these shores is a disaster and help will be needed. Always take money in the form of traveller's cheques rather than in sterling which is desirable throughout Europe and Asia. A good selection of credit cards is also a good idea.

When driving, it is possible to take pretty well all your tackle. Remember that you will not be able to get what you want abroad and even the simplest items like hooks or swivels can be impossible to locate. Also, take all types of gear, not just the big fish stuff. There can be exciting smaller fish along the way, for example nase, in central Europe. Personally, I would never travel abroad without fly tackle as well.

Take precautions against illness. Beware of the very hot sun, for heat can be insidious and you can find that you have sunstroke like never before. There is pain and shivering and sickness. Be careful of water outside western Europe. If going outside Europe check also on the injections necessary and wherever you travel do not get riotously drunk any of the time, but especially in the heat.

Remember to adapt to conditions. The information gleaned from friends, magazines or books may not always be accurate. This is not to say that they intend to mislead, but obviously things change. For example, the big reservoirs of Europe can fill dramatically after a storm, rise twenty or thirty feet and not be recognizable as the lake from which a friend caught fish. Human influences can also play a part. I fished on a Balkan lake which I reached after 1,300 hot miles during a national holiday. Never did I think I would be carp fishing in a massive holiday camp.

A distressing English chauvinist habit is to think that we invented fishing and we can put every other angler in the world to rights. Local anglers do know a thing or two about their own waters and I have been out-fished in the 1960s by boys with rods and reels that Woolworths would not have stocked. Yet they used the local method and I did not catch anything. It is as simple as that.

It is ridiculous to travel to a foreign country without a phrase book and a dictionary. You cannot rely on English being spoken outside France, the Low Countries, Germany and Austria. In the wilder area of the Balkans or Asia or the Iberian Peninsula it is rare. At the very least, learn the currency, the numbers, the simple food terms and the names of fish. With these, and a certain amount of arm waving, some information can be exchanged.

It is very easy to spend all your time travelling and never settling, always following a red–hot tip. In my experience, the truth is that foreign fishing is not unlike British sport – you have got to work hard at it to reap rewards. Very little will come easily either here or abroad. Big fish need work here, there and everywhere and you often need to build up a swim to get through the smaller fish. My advice is to get there, to settle, to learn and to develop your knowledge of the water. Successes should then build up but it is important to give yourself enough time. If at the planning stage you think you need five days then allow ten. If you think a week is enough, budget for two weeks and so on. Otherwise life gets hectic, you panic, and failure is guaranteed.

Even in comparative failure the best attitude is one of acceptance. Watch what goes on around you, enjoy it and appreciate all the fish that come your way. Put aside the mania for monsters – after all they are only the ones that make the headlines. Not all carp have to be galleons to be beautiful. Not all catfish need three people to support them to be worth catching. Smaller fish can be exciting and can make a holiday. For example, on the banks of Lake Bled in northern Yugoslavia, I saw some beautiful rudd that I tried but still failed to catch. But I enjoyed the whole affair, especially as the restaurant was close by and the bands were playing as evening fell. Lights flowed off the fairy-tale castle and glittered over the still water. So if you do go, enjoy it all and don't martyr yourself to the cause of monsters that may or may not come along.

If, however, they do come along, it pays dividends to make sure that you are capable of landing them. You are on the water and you are well.

INTRODUCTION

You have the bait and the tackle and the developing know-how to catch fish. Perhaps a carp now on your line doubles your previous personal best and is knocking 60lb. It could be that this is the catfish you always dreamed of, into three figures. This, then, is the moment of truth. Can you and your gear cope? The line, hooks, swivels, rods and reels that suffice for a 20lb fish do not always hold 70-pounders. Buy the very best and the very strongest before you go. Check if the shore line is rocky and if you will need a boat. Is your net up to landing something four or five feet long? Are your partners prepared to wade in and cradle a fish ashore? Have you got scales that go to 100lb plus if weight is vital to you? All these points could seem obvious but one tiny thing overlooked can often be the undoing of the entire trip.

Finally, once you are across the borders or over the seas don't let standards drop. We have all heard stories of Cassein frolics. Please do not poach but get tickets. If there is no night fishing allowed, then do not do it. If there are wildlife sanctuaries on the water then avoid them. If you want to drink heavily then do it in the privacy of your tent. If you have litter then take it home or to a bin. Be pleasant to the locals and they will virtually always help you unless they have had a bad experience with an English angler before. There is a trekking phrase that goes, 'Leave nothing but footsteps; take nothing but photographs'. It is a maxim that anglers abroad and in this country would do very well to follow.

1
Ferox – The Trail Continues

Many of those people kind enough to read *In Wild Waters* showed their interest in ferox, the great predatorial brown trout of the Scottish and Irish lochs. This strain of wild trout had been enthusiastically pursued up until the 1930s and had then been largely forgotten about apart from chance captures through the efforts of men like Bill Keale, Fred Wagstaffe and Ray Brown in the late 1960s and early 1970s. My own fascination with these little-known giants of the vast waters began as a child but it was to be many years on before I had the time, money and experience to pursue them in earnest. Then I was to find ferox to be the most difficult fish I had ever attempted. In those lochs that hold them, ferox are invariably few in number. They live in huge, deep, wild waters. Little is known of their erratic feeding habits at largely unknown depths and times. I had to learn boat control and the whole art of lure fishing. Every ferox trip required over fifteen hundred miles of travelling and demanded money, time, pain and dedication. At my lowest ebb – and there were many of them – the ferox seemed quite an impossible mission.

Roger Miller was my companion in the early days when we found our base camp at the Dick Down Hotel and made our first faltering attempts for ferox. *In Wild Waters* was written at the end of that initial phase. I still had to boat a decent fish at the time and perhaps should not have written the section in the book as I did. However, my aim was to convey the excitement we both felt and to at least smooth over some of the problems for those willing to suffer a similar apprenticeship.

When *In Wild Waters* went to the publishers, I knew that my ferox dreams were almost completely unrealized. I had made a start on the species and that was exciting but the fish still remained to be caught. I was back, therefore, at Dick Down in late October 1988, too late to fish for ferox but intent on watching and echo-sounding their spawning areas. It

A fine Irish trout dwarfs the spoon that caught it.

was a successful trip and one of great beauty. By then there was already snow on the hills and the deer rut was at its climax. At the head of one river I watched two stags fight for over an hour before the loser broke off and fled over the hill line. It was at that same place that I saw my first major ferox. It had swum miles, I guess to spawn in the fast gravels, and there it had been trapped along with salmon to be stripped by the fishery board.

It would be easy for me to was wax lyrical about the fish – and didn't I do just that in the bar that night! But I will restrict myself to factual observation. The ferox was quite as majestic as older writers had lead me to believe. It was very solid, very dark coloured, with bold markings. Unfortunately the fish was not weighed and a discussion frequently flared up around its size that I privately put around 14lb. As I have since witnessed on many other ferox, the adipose fin was abnormally large and certainly not the emasculated stump common to stewpond rainbows. There could be little doubt that the fish was in pristine condition and it completely gave the lie to the often-stated belief that ferox are mean, lanky, big-headed beasts on their last fins. This one must have had years of life left in it – or would have had if the shock of capture and handling had not, I believe, eventually lead to its death.

In the rapid water, both trout and char can be found come autumn.

Inspired then, by the knowledge that ferox did exist, I appeared as the first resident of the Dick Down Hotel in March 1989. It was a period of savage weather and the hotel was cut off for three days by blizzards. In the bothy next to the hotel, fellow ferox hunter John MacDonald was staying in temperatures well below freezing in order to be out on the water early. He caught fish steadily up to a couple of pounds but the really large ferox evaded him and me both. During a severe squall, when I was playing a decent fish and leaning out to net it, a storm force gust turned the boat turtle and I lost half my gear and – I believed for a second – would have lost my life. It was a shock and a sobering reminder of how desperately dangerous a gale on a ten-mile-long piece of water can become.

The weather improved and so did ferox fortunes. Right at the end of the month, though bitterly cold and windy still, Norrie, the giant builder from Edinburgh, and his friend John ventured out on to Mansion Loch. On my advice, John was brave enough to troll with a dead rainbow trout. For me the bait had not worked but for him, within twenty-five minutes, he returned with a lovely $8\frac{1}{2}$lb trout. Once more the ferox lay before me and I spent an hour examining it. Its tail had a vast spread and its jaw held

A period of blizzards!

quite enough teeth to justify our use of wire traces. Once more the adipose fin struck me hugely. It was vast, almost an extra fin and in no way the stumpy appendage stuck on stockie rainbows. There were also a few red spots sprinkled among the galaxies of black ones. Only now could I question that nineteenth-century belief that the ferox was black-spotted. Perhaps this is so in certain lochs but its validity as a general rule of ferox identification I now began to question.

May came and I began to concentrate more on natural baits than artificial in those parts of the lochs where there was the strongest current or drift. After several small fish of up to 4lb or so, it became my belief that a ferox could well wait in a position for food to be carried to it and from where it would rarely need to stray either far or often. So this proved on the 28th of the month. Then, my half trout, which I trotted down a long deep run at the head of a loch, was seized. Again I must be careful not to dwell on the excitement of the fight that lasted overly long because of my timidity and because of the remarkable power and resilience of the fish. At long last, it came out at $30\frac{3}{4}$in long and $10\frac{1}{2}$lb in weight. Very shortly elation became tragedy. I put the fish in a carp sack while I went to the Dick Down for cameras and witnesses. When I returned, only thirty minutes later, the flow of water had diminished and the sack hung limp.

A wild hind comes to be fed in the cold spring.

Imagine falling into this.

One of the first big ferox.

The fish, I felt sure, would recover and hurried pictures were taken. Between 6 p.m. and 8.10 p.m. I and John Hett took turns to hold the fish in the full flow before it went away groggily into the loch. The following morning I found it dead, washed back into the shore, in part already consumed by eels.

I blamed myself bitterly. The incident did serve to show how hard this wildest of fish takes to any form of captivity. Future experiences confirm that after only a couple of minutes a fish can begin to discolour from shock. Once this happens its life is in jeopardy. Only once again, in Ireland, would I sack a ferox, and many potentially good shots were, of necessity, sacrificed for the good of this very rare fish.

Dick Down as a Spiritual Home

When I wrote my recent book, *The Great Anglers*, I listed the late B.B. as my own personal, greatest angling writer. It is gratifying to find that nigh on thirty years ago B.B. himself discovered the paradise that is 'my' ferox glen. He wrote of his experience there in *Creel* magazine and I include it now as something of a tribute to his memory.

Morning in Paradise

B.B.

To find oneself on the shores of a lovely West Highland Loch, with a boat within a few yards of the caravan, superb fishing ground on the far side, a mile away, and being held powerless by the weather, that was my fortune in early June of this year! I had gone up north from the Midlands with the set purpose of catching a ferox, a fish which has always exercised a powerful fascination for me since reading the accounts of St John and Macdonald Robertson. These huge lake trout rarely take a fly (though I saw a fine specimen in the Dick Down Hotel which was caught in a nearby loch).

The evening we arrived a heat-wave was just finishing, the loch lay like blue glass under the stern and wooded hills. It was so warm, in fact, we stripped and swam off-shore where the shingle dived down into awesome deeps, black as ebony.

We were so confident that first evening, that we never went out in the boat but fished the mouth of a burn hard by camp where I caught a fine brown trout for breakfast.

But I knew it was on the far side that the best fish lay, just off a mysterious shore of white sand and thick alder groves where a wooded island jutted forth – once the nesting site of the proud ospreys.

But, alas, for such confidence! Next morning the skies were grey, the winds blew, and the erstwhile blue mirror was now a churning mass of grey water and white waves breaking.

And so it went on, for most of my precious week, the wind blowing so fierce and rough that no boat could safely live in the waves and we even had to persuade the head keeper to find us a more sheltered pitch, where the violence of the gales could not reach us.

And then, one morning, two days before we were due to return upon the long road south, I awoke soon after dawn and found a morning in Paradise! The lock lay sleeping without a ripple, ringed here and there by small troutlings. The mountains round, all showing snowfields around their crest even in June (a thing never remembered, so I was told, by the local men of the hills), some reflected in the still mirror, and eastwards the sun was rising in an unsullied sky.

I pushed off in the boat and soon was chugging across to the far delectable shore. I put out a Devon on my trolling rod and headed for Osprey Island. Its dark firs were reflected faithfully, upside down, in the water, a reflection which was broken into a thousand pieces by the furl of my wake.

For half an hour I gently coasted down the shore, disturbing a red deer which was wading in the water by a little grove of alder and birch.

I was some 300 yards off-shore and still heading west when the point of the trolling rod went down and the reel screamed.

Then followed the most exciting half-hour of my angling life, for I was fishing with a very light spinning rod and a 6lb breaking strain line.

The fish never showed itself but tore in every direction with a long steady pull.

The battle went on, past Osprey Island, until the shingle spit hove was in sight where our

An angry loch at night fall.

caravan was berthed, and still my fish played deep. Was it a salmon, a ferox, or a big sea-trout? I could not tell. But the battle having waged from the centre of the loch to the home shore, I gave a loud hallo to awake the ladies. They responded nobly, tumbling out of the van like scared hens, and as I jumped ashore with the rod they grabbed the landing net.

Then a bar of silver leapt and gleamed. It was, alas, no ferox, but a fine sea-trout of 6lb. With two days still to go before returning home my hopes were high for bigger fish, but the weather broke once more, the hateful wind came back and never again could I make the passage to the far side. Mountainous waves careered down the loch, funnelled, no doubt, by the steep glens around.

But it had been worth travelling over six hundred miles to experience that early morning battle, when all the world was so clear and still, and the only active thing, my line, cutting purposefully here and there in the black waters of the loch.

Learning More about the Ferox

Very often in the last couple of years I have been asked whether the ferox is a distinct strain of brown trout or simply an ordinary brown trout grown predatorial and therefore large. Over a century ago, the Victorians thought that the ferox was this distinct strain but then from the 1940s the scientific mood changed. Then it became the common belief that ferox were nothing more than big cannibal trout. Today, however, the tide has

A big ferox with points of recognition in a book above it.

A magnificent autumn run ferox.

The ferox spawning river.

A perfect brown of 2½lb – on the way to being a big fish.

turned again. The more recent belief is that ferox have the ability to grow for fifteen to eighteen years, compared with the normal brown trout's life span of a mere five to seven years. Length of growing life appears to be the key to ferox's success in the loch.

It certainly seems that ferox spawn quite apart from other fish and have their own distinct redds, come the autumn. I have, in fact, talked to three different people who have seen a legion of ferox in the act of spawning. The spawning ground is a well-known one and is situated where a loch empties in to a fast, boulder-strewn river. My witnesses have all confirmed that the ferox gather there in the fast water towards late October. Estimates of the numbers of fish vary from between thirty to fifty, all big ferox, all pushing and vying for position. A bridge gives a perfect vantage place and the onlookers could get a very accurate idea of the length and, importantly, the breadth of the fish beneath them. By all three men, the smaller fish were estimated to weight between 5 and 8lb. The very few largest were 25lb plus! It must have been a staggering sight. Presuming this behaviour to be typical, it would seem that ferox always breed with ferox and that the fry possess the special qualities of their massive parents.

I have personally been present during the autumn push of ferox into spawning rivers and streams. Some time late in September, it seems that the loch's population is on the move, drifting to the appointed faster water. During this period, the fish are very aggressive indeed, taking baits with savagery. Never are they more ferocious or, once located, more easily caught. In the autumns of 1989 and 1990 I witnessed a depressing slaughter of smaller ferox in the 5–8lb bracket – fish that I felt generally should have been returned, unharmed, to the water. I am not alone in believing that the ferox populations of all lochs are low and an autumn kill-off can have severe repercussions. In fact, a very detailed research programme on one ten-mile loch by a Scottish university, estimated that the entire ferox population was only between twenty and thirty fish, weighing up to a maximum of possibly 22lb. In such a large and deep water it is inevitable that some fish were missed by the sonar beams but a couple of fish per square mile seems to be a typical ferox count. Considering that only around 150 lochs hold ferox, there could be possibly around only 4,000 individuals alive at present today in the Highlands. This must make then the rarest of indigenous UK species and reinforce the need for their protection.

I have already told of the death of my $10\frac{1}{2}$lb fish.

Even a 5 or 6lb fish will fight close to the boat for upwards of ten minutes at times and, if allowed, will dive to depths of forty feet repeatedly. The wear and tear of a battle like this on a fish must be enormous. Once boated, the ferox obviously reacts equally badly to handling. It is essential that matting or wet sacking, perhaps a wetted carp sack, is available to place the fish upon. Forceps, scales and cameras must all be prepared for the arrival of the fish. From my increasing experience it would appear that any ferox kept out of water for more than three or four minutes is very probably a dead one. The first signs of a very badly suffering fish are the patches of discolouration along the back and flanks. The fish breathes hard at first and then hardly at all while this deterioration increases rapidly. Avoid it.

Upon return, the fish is very likely to need a fair amount of nursing. Do not put the fish back and let go immediately for it could plummet down yard upon yard into the cold black water, to die there. Rather hold it in the surface layers waiting for strength to return, for the power to ripple along the flanks and for it to forge away across the surface under its own power. Once of the most inspiring sights I ever saw was one bright day when Pete Rogers expertly played, landed, unhooked, photographed and returned a big fish. Even though the whole process was done as swiftly as

A lovely ferox for Peter Rogers – Don Wheeler is the photographer.

possible the fish needed holding for a minute before it surged away beneath us, hit the bottom at about fifteen feet and disappeared like a massive mahogany bullet into the depths.

When writing *In Wild Waters*, and indeed right until late 1989, I stuck by the time-honoured belief that rough weather was necessary for ferox hunting. 'Choose the roughest weather that your boat can live in' became a motto that cost me hardship and nearly my life and produced very few fish indeed. Those ferox that were caught in calm, bright conditions I steadfastly put down to chance. Then, little by little, light dawned. Of course, ferox are caught in dirty weather but very many are taken in good weather also. In fact, despite being afloat whatever the conditions, it appears that sixty to seventy per cent of my action – and that of others – came in pleasant or at least settled weather. I know a fly-fisher likes a good blow but when boat control becomes a chore then I feel my ferox chances are slipping.

The age-old ferox fisher's obsession appears to be getting the bait or the lure down deep and indeed on the Humminbird screen it often appears that big fish are lying at fifty feet and below. It would seem obvious that a deep-worked bait stands a better chance of being taken, yet over the years I became worried by the number of fish taken by, can we say, amateur

Once considered poor conditions, now we favour bright, still days. Norrie takes a break.

A fine ferox falls to a shallow-run bait.

trollers, trailing baits at ten feet or above. Again, I realized that there was a limit to how many of these fish could be written off as flukes.

One day I was working two lures, one at thirty feet and one at twelve feet. The higher lure landed fish of 3lb and 8lb while the lower one was not touched all day long. Then I began to look clearly at the fish positions on the Humminbird. Often the bigger shapes were close to the bottom at fifty feet plus but then, quite frequently, a large fish would be well up off the bottom lying at between fifteen and twenty-five feet. These observations began to suggest to me that resting fish lie deep, on or near the bottom, but that feeding fish become active and rise in the water, searching out their prey nearer to the surface. This theory was strengthened by observation. Increasingly I began to go out in calm conditions from dawn to dusk and I began to watch the water more often that the echo-sounder screen. Time after time, I spotted big fish on the surface, striking or merely swimming in the surface layers. It was around this time of new experience that, using live baits, a 12lb fish took a small trout at fifteen feet while two others, fished at thirty and forty feet respectively, were ignored.

While the question of depth has, for me, become less important, the necessity to be out as many hours as possible has grown. I see no pattern of feeding times emerging at all. The dawn is good but so is late morning, early afternoon and our own tea-time. It seems that a ferox or two can rise up to the light at almost any time of the day and a take can come literally out of the blue. You simply have to be there when a fish decides to feed. But note I am not saying that lead core lines and down-riggers do not produce fish. What I am stressing is that they are not strictly necessary; can you imagine being alone in a boat in a strong wind when the cannonball of the down-rigger snags on the bottom at over sixty feet depth?

Any pike angler who watches a ferox surface to feed will have to conclude that the trout is not an efficient hunter of small fish. Anything up to four or five strikes are often needed before a fish takes its meal from a large char shoal. I watched one especially large fish go quite manic among a shoal of smutting char before it made a kill and the loch settled again. It churned into the shoal over and over, working up speed and literally thrashing the water to a foam. When the fish disappeared and the char reassembled 200 yards away I concluded that the ferox had been successful although I could not swear to that. The apparent inefficiency of ferox hunting is good news for the angler. It probably means that ferox has to prowl quite a while to ensure its food and it must make a tethered bait seem a relatively easy target.

I should stress the excitement of actually seeing ferox on the top when for years I could hardly believe that they even existed. It was as though I were making the most astonishing breakthrough, especially when I realized that almost always when I saw one ferox, I would see three or four others if visibility allowed. Where there was one ferox there were generally others, hunting together almost perch-like in a loose shoal. Ferox a shoal fish! Never had I read that, but I was to confirm it again especially when livebaiting. Then, if one bait went, almost certainly others would follow before the feeding spell was at an end.

Improvements in Methods

In Wild Waters contained a good deal of what I still believe to be sound advice on trolling, the primary method for catching ferox. However, two years of very hard work since then have inevitably lead to various changes of approach. My views on tackle have advanced a little, especially

The majesty of ferox jaws in 1890.

regarding line choice. For quite a while I have been using a brand monofilament which was excellent in its resistance to abrasion and which gave pleasing visibility when it was close to propellers and other danger areas. The trouble was I feared that the fish just might be able to see the line equally well. This worry has been echoed by the American book, *Environmental Physics.* 'In every instance the fluorescent lines were easily seen and photographed under water. They glowed in the water as readily as above, and when viewed under water against backgrounds of contrasting colours, actually seemed to glow more intensely. The easiest to see and photograph were the lines with a fluorescent yellow or orange quality . . . At ten feet away, the lines were highly visible and actually seemed to be much larger in diameter, as if surrounded by a halo of glowing light.'

[29]

'The line must be 15lb breaking strain and no less.' *(In Wild Waters.)* Partly as a result of this American research I decided to settle in the future on neutral coloured lines with as thin a diameter as I could safely use. I now believe that in crystal-clear lochs even plain lines are always visible to the very sharp-eyed predators and it pays handsomely to reduce the diameter as much as feasible. The second reason for using lighter lines in, say, the 8–11lb category is that they allow lures to work significantly more deeply than lines in the 15–20lb class. The extra resistance of heavier lines automatically pulls the lures up higher in the water. Of course, it goes without saying that these lighter lines are more suceptible to wear and need frequent checking. I have found that it makes sense to fill the spool to within a quarter inch of the brim with heavy line and then top up with a hundred yards of approximately 10lb line that can frequently be replaced from a bulk spool.

Obviously, the use of a trace continues to be essential. More controversially, I am totally happy now with Olympic Kevlar trace material which I find resilient, soft and blissfully easy to tie up. I hear there are those with unhappy experiences of the product but I am not one.

'The question of reels is easily solved. Multipliers are simply a must.' *(In Wild Waters.)* When I lost the multipliers overboard in the storm I

A small, but beautifully shaped ferox.

[30]

needed to restock with reels. I was introduced to the Shimano Bait Runners as a possible alternative. I bought one to start with and after only two days trolling sent down for two more. The bait runner facility is absolutely perfect for the trolling game. The spool is large enough to take any line capacity needed, reeling in is quick and easy and if casting is ever necessary a fixed spool wins over the multiplier with lighter baits. For me anyway, the multiplier is now obsolete. I choose the larger size of bait runner and an quite happy with the 4500 GT.

'The rods we use are powerful pike-type weapons with $2\frac{1}{2}$ or 3lb test curve.' (*In Wild Waters*.) I would now modify this statement. I have seen lighter, delicate nine foot rods used for lures and their sensitivity does seem to be a definite advantage. They have a feel that the more pokey type tools lack. If this is possible, they seem to divine the action of the lure in the take of a fish at a hundred yards range and thirty feet depth. Even for deadbait trolling, I now have a misgiving about a traditional pike rod. Something softer that offers less resistance to a take seems advisable. I have had baits dropped by fish feeling the resistance of an overly stiff rod and takes are still so occasional that you really do not want to miss them when they happen.

'Almost anything can take a fish; big 'S' plugs have worked; Rapala lures a success; Tobys – especially silver and bronze and copper ones are also favourites; A big fish from Loch Laggan was recently taken on a small Mepps. In short, most plugs, spoons and spinners are worth an extended trial.' (*In Wild Waters*.) This is all true but so dismissive that now I wince. Two years and several hundred trolled miles on I still don't feel really qualified to advise. It is one thing to say authoritatively which lures work at what depths but it is quite a different matter to state what a ferox will actually take. However, since spending a week with Pete Rogers and Don Wheeler, my liking is now for plugs, large ones of the Kwikfish and Flatfish varieties that work deep and energetically and have moved plenty of fish. These plugs are very easy to use, do not need weights or lead core lines and keep around twenty-five to thirty-two feet down depending on boat speed, line diameter and distance trailed behind the boat. Takes are not always the savage, rod-wrenching affairs that you would initially expect and it pays to watch the rod tip and strike as quickly as possible.

Livebaiting for Ferox

This is not to say I have not livebaited for ferox but I will add at once that livebaiting for them is not, in my view, ethical. The ferox, really should

Who is afraid of whom?

be caught on a lure bait but there are times when a live bait seems the only practical answer. Some fish get so used to seeing spinners and plugs over a number of years that a take from them really would be an aberration. In these cases, perhaps, a live bait is just about advisable and justifiable.

Of course, it would be quite wrong to import live baits. To bring coarse fish up for the job in Loch Lomond pike style would be utterly wrong. Small trout should be bought from fish farms that are on the loch or be caught from the feeder streams of the loch. I am not even happy about this latter solution as a lot of loch trout populations are on the way down.

Nor is livebaiting for ferox nearly as easy as it would at first sound or seem. These ferox waters are vast, with low ferox populations, and to fish static baits would be to risk very long waits indeed. Trolling live baits is a possibility but you would have to cover water slowly and not much ground would be tried. Probably, the strongest possibility is to livebait if and when you think you have located a ferox group – though of course this could move – and when it seems that the fish reject all manner of lures. All my experience goes to suggest that ferox do not take a bait at all in the manner of a pike. Anything other than the big male ferox has a smaller, narrower head than that of even an 8lb jack and it takes that much longer for the bait to be engulfed. That suggests that a longer time should be given to a taking ferox. In theory! In practice, I suspect the trout has a more sensitive mouth than the pike. Probably its life as an insect feeder leads it to greater discrimination. Certainly, the trout I have encountered have not held on to a bait nearly as long as a pike would have done. The other point to bear in mind is that a pike on a typical water seizes a bait and needs only to dive between one and ten feet to reach the bottom. The ferox, however, probably comes up forty, eighty or a hundred-plus feet for its attack and on the return, the resistance of the float must increase steadily on this sensitive fish.

In short then, piking experience must be discounted. Certainly, I have found ferox in the 6–15lb category closer to perch in their feeding habits, or perhaps zander, a fish I personally have no knowledge of. Resistance has got to be kept to a minimum. Greased lines, small streamlined floats, baits in the 3–5 inch category, small, sharp, strong hooks, constant observation and quick striking are all very necessary if the ferox is to be hooked. For all these reasons, livebaiting in a biggish wave is difficult. The float is lost in a trough, the bait is taken unseen, the rod whips round and back again and the ferox is alarmed and away. Even the resistance of the line clip or the loosest bait runner is enough to scare the predator off.

Livebaiting for ferox can be the peak of excitement – the steely dawn when the loch is pewter still. A dorsal cutting the surface, shark-like, and further away a strike into a shoal of surface-dimpling char. Two red floats working against a backdrop of peaks and forests, I pull very slightly on the oars, little more than drifting down the drop-off that shows on the echo-sounder. Both floats become agitated. One lies flat as the bait rises in the water. It moves rapidly to the left, cocks, sinks and the line flows from the reel. I ship the oars, stand up, tighten and strike into what I know is a good fish. Like most, it comes in close to the boat without protest. Ten yards away it wakes up to this unguessed danger and spins off wildly down into eighty feet of water. Though the reel screams the hooks are not set properly and I lose what I know is a big fish. Fingers tremble. My mouth too dry for curses. I fumble for another bait, recast and row slowly back over the same area. A float lies flat. Seconds pass and still it is horizontal. Rod in hand I stand in the boat. Five yards beyond the float the bait is on the surface, swimming madly away from me. Immediately a giant ferox head emerges behind it, snapping and swirling at the desperate fish. Its back, its tail, two feet of its body are plainly visible as it harries the tiny rainbow trout. This fish is 14lb minimum, it could be more. A lot

A huge ferox.

more. I tense for a strike as the big fish disappears from my view. The float does not move. There was no take. The big angry ferox had missed its mark or seen danger at the last second.

Fifteen minutes on and for the third time a float goes. Line running. Within a minute the fish is leaping around the boat. Eight times it leaps a yard or more in the air and a deep run follows. When it surfaces again, it is beaten fish: 10lb 2oz. Brown as a tench and just a few big black spots scattered as if with a random brush down its flank.

It is 5 p.m. and the autumn day has a chill to it now that the rain has stopped, the wind has died and a cold blue sky has spread from the mountains from the west to the forests of the east. The Dick Down calls me home.

Flossie's Last Morning

Flossie was the hotel dog. In all probability she loved the river even more than the fisherman that she followed down to it for so many years of her

A Spaniel study.

long life. As you fished, she snuffled out stones in the margins, often disappearing down to her tail for a minute or more. She grew old, she became fat, hearing gone, eyesight dimmed, arthritic in joint. Her teeth were worn away to nothing by a lifetime of stone grubbing and yet she lived on. Inspired by the river. By a zest for the glen.

Late in September, I rose just before dawn. There was a frost and the way down to the valley floor was hazardous. Before I reached it Flossie was with me, breathless, complaining that I had left without her. On the point of daybreak I was fishing and she was stoning. I took a char first cast and then the dawn took me over. It was so magical all I could do was watch it flood into the world. I like to think that Flossie saw it too, head briefly out of water and tired eyes focusing on the east.

Breakfast time. We made our way up the valley side. Hard for me and a trial for Flossie. A short time later a car that she could not hear reversed and broke her leg.

She was buried in a piece of land to the west, towards a church, where, even kneeling down, you can see the midday sunshine glint on the rapids way below.

Hector A. MacDonald

The greatest angler the long history of the glen has ever known was Hector A. MacDonald. Cased fish after cased fish bears the legend that he was 'the notable gillie'. Today, MacDonald's family still lives in the village at the foot of the valley and the stories about him so abound that it is hard to believe that he has been dead for so many seasons.

He lived at the Dick Down when the hotel was a farm, a garage, a post office and the telephone exchange as well as a place to stay. He was the prince of a whole team of gillies who served the sportsmen of the early- and mid-century. Then, only paying-guests entered through the front doors of the hotel and the grooms, the glenmen and the gillies all used the rough bar that is still in part standing at the rear of the hotel, among the bothies, sheds and stores. There, night after night, season after season, Hector A. MacDonald held sway. Every salmon lie. Every hill lochan. Every twist in the burns. Every drop away in the lochs. He knew them all. He was a beautiful caster, a crack shot, a sinuous oarsman. He was the personification of sport in the glen and often had scant respect for those who employed him. He could be truculent. He invariably took credit for any capture. It was said you didn't trust him with a bottle or a girl but he

Hector A. MacDonald holds a 10lb trout.

was always forgiven and revered for his knowledge and love of the glen. Nothing could keep him away from it.

The war came. Hector's shooting skill was needed. He was captured and sent to work in a Silesian mine. There eventually he feigned blindness. The Germans put him through every test, often painful, and he never flinched. Finally, defeated, they shipped him home and he landed at Southampton, still 'blind'. The Government took him back to his glen and gave him a pension for life. Once the bureaucrats' backs were turned, Hector, blind as an eagle, continued his work as before. To the end of his days Hector could 'see a dram on a mountain top five miles away'. Nothing could or would keep Hector from his life's love.

The Dick Down Pine Marten

'There is nothing they can't do,' he said, 'they can swim like otters, climb like squirrels, run like rabbits. They eat anything, are almost impossible to trap and they have outwitted virtually every stalker in the glen.'

'How come they are so rare?' I asked.

Splendid evening light, over a ferox loch.

'Ah now,' mine host said conspiratorially, 'there's just that one thing they're no good at, at all!'

Since childhood I had wanted to see a pine marten and now I heard of this one being fed at the back of the hotel. Sausage, chicken, toast and jam were its favourite dishes and night after night the waitresses went scurrying out to fill up its larder on the bird table. It was easy to see where it ate, where it slept and where it ran . . . everything but the animal itself. When I slept in the bothy I heard it attack the fledglings. Then I moved into the hotel and chose a back room that overlooked the yard. Always though, I seemed to go to sleep too early or wake too late to catch sight of this most cunning of animals. Like Pooh Bear with the tantalizing Heffalump, I began to become irritated. I had even been as mad as to hope for a photograph and the camera had stood unfired on its tripod for two and a half weeks.

I was shaken awake. A naked Miller towered over me. 'It's there.' I needed no further prompting. In the gloom of the courtyard below I could see the flow of the animal, surprising large, rippling over the gravel, up the sheds at last to the bird table on which the camera was trained and focused. I depressed the release bulb. The animal heard the shutter fall from a full fifteen yards and was gone in a blur of dawn. I never saw the creature again. Not even in a photograph. That single frame was pitch black but for a perfectly shaped, white question mark of blurred activity.

A Plague of Bats

My first stay at the Dick Down coincided with a most peculiar episode. Not that in any way the hotel could be blamed. A premature burst of spring weather had lured the pipistrelle bats from the attic and some sixty odd of the creatures had flown down into the hotel where they again sought a secure hibernation when the weather turned colder. They appeared in the beds, in shoes, amongst clothes, in the dining room and even in a matchbox. A woman screamed when she found one in a tin of oatcakes at breakfast time. A man jokingly claimed compensation for two pinpricks on his jugular! When any member of the hotel appeared, it was furtively, hands cupped, on the way up to the roof space. One of the last bats to go was the one that lodged in my dirty socks. I tried to feed him little insects but he grew more and more tired and at last I took him back to his family in the loft. Then they, and the whole hotel, settled down in peace at last.

Sporting Lives

Farquar is in the glen, home again from Australia. He returns every years to lead the stalking in these hills that he has known since infancy. He is a fisherman too and this season, and last, like the ones before, the majority of the salmon have been caught by Farquar because he feels for the river like he does for the hills. Men have watched him from high in the birch woods. He fishes runs where they know there are no lies and they have laughed behind their binoculars. Then he catches salmon and like the wolf in *Little Red Riding Hood* they gnash their teeth in silent fury.

Alan is his friend from boyhood. Both are quietly and gently alike with a twinkle in their eyes that is as sunlight reflected from the burns. Though an autumn wind sighs in the upper glen, Alan has seen a trout rise and he keeps on with the dry fly even though it is drowned in the sleet now and then. At the very last he catches his trout.

Over the line of hills from him there is a house party at The Lodge. Wine flows at the five-course dinners each night and the team of stalkers and gillies meets in the yard after each lavish breakfast. By late afternoon tea is served in front of the roaring fire and there will be two stags in the

Enjoyment, Dick Down style.

[40]

A superbly shaped ferox.

outhouse and three salmon and six brace of grouse in the larder. Above, the boilers are steaming to prepare bath water for a dozen and the cook sweats in the kitchen to ensure the venison will melt in the sauce.

Down the glen, four lads wait in the rain for the breakdown truck. Their car came off the single-track road at a bend, breaking the fuel line and half a dozen fishing rods. They have sat through four days of solid rain and wind, and late last night, the stove left on, burned down their tent. The boy who woke scalded his arm putting out the blaze. Four days, four fishermen and not a fish to show for it.

The backpacker walking for five days in the wilderness; the naturalist tracking the high-ground otters; the photographer on the cliff face below the eyrie at dawn; the lone ferox troller, a dot on the huge loch: the glen is sport for all.

The Char Boom

My initial interest in char was simply as ferox food. Trailing the shoals on the Humminbird fish finder was an interesting way to the door of the ferox and little more. The char, we knew, was a small fish and we did not think them particularly interesting to catch. Indeed, the 4lb 13oz char on the wall of the Dick Down Bar seemed as unattainable as the similarly coloured rainbow. To Miller and me in those early days, that fish seemed to be a freak, a one off and unrepeatable miracle. Naturally it was not. Nature does not throw up a single massive fish and that huge char had to have its peers.

In our glen, and neighbouring ones, 1989 and 1990 produced successions of massive char. Three pounders – once potential record-breakers – have become common and even four pounders are no longer the champagne fish they once were. As I write now in the Dick Down lounge, a 4lb 7oz char hangs over my head in its gorgeous case. It was caught in May 1989 and at that time was the second biggest UK char. Now I doubt if it would make the top ten!

The first revelation about a true twist in the history of char fishing took place in the third week of September 1989. I was actually awakened in England at 2 a.m. on Sunday 23 September by a phone call from a wild Welshman 600 miles to the north telling me the news. I could hardly take in what he said then or even later. The gist was that in a clutch of short sessions, four Englishmen had landed several 3 and 4lb char including a mass of 2lb-plus fish. A vast shoal had moved out of the loch up a feeder

Another mighty char.

river in their search for the spawning beds. They had settled there in the fast water and had taken Mepps spinners madly, either out of hunger, or more likely, territorial aggression. The fish, apparently, were 'queuing up' for the lures and were, sadly, all killed by the good souls who mistook them for grilse. The anglers were not alone in reaping a bonanza. One of them heard a rustling in the bracken that grew close to the ever-growing pile of fish. He approached carefully and found an otter at dinner over his catch!

The early season of 1990 saw even greater things. I arrived in the North to the rumour of a 5lb plus char that had fallen to the lure of ferox man, John McDonald. Our own great day arrived in May, as we trolled along the deep south shore of a deep, slightly choppy loch. Midday approached and Joy had the rods when a fish took the five-inch Flatfish plug, travelling at twenty-five to thirty feet down. She played the fish for a while and handed me the rod for an opinion. I agreed with her that it felt like a good-sized trout, and I was about to hand back the rod when ten or fifteen feet below the float I saw the flash of white – edged pectorals that could only mean char. I also saw the shadowy size of the fish. 'Joy,' I said, quite calmly, 'we've broken the char record!' So, for a while, it proved.

[43]

Our short-lived char record.

From 4lb 13oz, the record moved to our own 5lb 9oz monster. Always I have wondered what it would be like to hold a record and to be named in the eternal halls of fame. For ten days this dream had become reality. Then rumours, soon to be proved correct, circulated the glens of a 6lb fish. Fame and fortune were fickle jades – for almost as quickly the record moved on to John McDonald again, with a 7lb fish!

In September 1990, once again the char trekked from the loch to their river-mouth spawning-beds and this time I met them myself. Along with other anglers, I caught fish steadily over a two-week period up to just over the 4lb mark. The period was notable for several things. It was the first time that I have fished so consistently for the species and I became ever more impressed by their looks, their fight and their caution – or at least by the vagaries of their behaviour. It seemed, and I stress seemed, that the char ran in shoals of between ten and thirty fish. These shoals were highly mobile, with members frequently rising, topping, rolling, and splashing on the surface over four to eight feet of water as they ran. It also appeared that char runs could happen at any time of the day and that the major movements of fish took place at dusk and dawn. Why not throughout the night too, we all wondered? Activity was particularly noticeable after a flood. There were two periods of heavy rain during the fortnight (typical Scottish wet periods of ninety-six hours non-stop stair-rodding) and this saw a lot of fish in the swollen river mouth. These char shoals held their position in quick water for short periods before dropping back to the upper loch. Almost certainly the fish were not yet spawning. It was quite easy to see them in the shallow water over the stones and they displayed none of the spawning activity that you would expect. My own belief is that they were simply sounding out the area ready to spawn later in the autumn.

It was hard to decide whether the fish were hungry by the way they attacked Mepps and other small spoons or whether they were simply territorial in the vicinity of their spawning redds. My guess is the latter. Many fish were not properly hooked but just bumped the lure as it passed them by. On those days that I wore polaroid sun-glasses and the sun was out, I would often see two or three fish following the lure to the bank, policing it out of harm's way. Those few fish that were killed were invariably empty of food and this suggested that feeding was temporarily suspended during the build up to the spawning period.

At the peak of all this activity, Andy, the bailiff of the glen, came into the bar one wet night to report his day's findings. Beneath a bridge, he and Sandy the forester had watched groups of char pass and repass the river mouth virtually all day long. They had landed char weighing up to around 4lb on silver spinners, and any other colour, they found, was ignored. They also discovered that the only taking periods were when the sun briefly shone. When the cloud and rain came back the fish disappeared and no more takes were registered. This tended to coincide with my own experience but much more excitingly they reported hooking one fish that was at least half as big again as the largest fish that they landed. It fought valiantly in the heavy flow of water for some while before simply opening its mouth and spitting the silver Mepps right out of the water. That fish they estimated could not weigh less than 6–7lb. That was not all. Whilst playing that fish they had seen through polaroid glasses a group of char following, puzzled and enormous. These fish were at least twice the size of the 4-pounder landed and noticeably larger than the fish on the line. In short, both men, both experienced anglers, were quire convinced that they had seen char in the 8–10lb bracket beneath them for a period that spanned several hours.

Of course, in Greenland the char feed in the sea and run up the rivers there to spawn, and these fish, when caught, are massive. They can weigh close on 30lb for they have the benefit of a lifetime of sea feeding. For a land-locked British char to weigh 10lb would be quite extraordinary.

A beautifully marked autumn-run ferox.

Consider the fact that for years the record was only 2 and then a meagre 3lb you will see the magnitude of these Scottish char. Indeed, a 10lb char would be the equivalent of a 12 or 15lb roach! The reasons behind this char explosion are unresearched. I have discussed the matter with Dr Barber, a fishery biologist in Scotland, and he seems quite convinced that this char boom is linked with the salmon cages on various lochs. On the majority of these super char waters, small salmon are raised intensively by commercial companies. It is Dr Barber's belief that the surplus pellets filter into the loch and boost char growth. Thereafter, a great many parr and smolts escape into the lochs to provide a further food source for quick-growing char. Very probably, Dr Barber's thesis is correct. The 5lb 9oz char that Joy and I landed in May 1990 unfortunately died. The free treble hook had caught in the fish's eye and during the fight had pulled this clean away. It was a tragic happening and I felt it better to kill a fish thus maimed. When the fish was gutted it was found to be full of exactly the food types that Dr Barber had surmised. The mixture in its stomach was a revolting one of half-digested pellets and five salmon parr, each around four inches in length.

Possibly, therefore, the char could become even larger if the salmon farms are allowed to continue. If the problems of disease, market or environmental conditions force them off, then presumably the char populations of these lochs will 'decline' back to their former insignificance. These char catches could be merely a temporary blip in the history of a species in this country.

How many large char each loch can hold is open to debate and sometimes this has been furious in the bar of the Dick Down at night. It is always tempting to overestimate the numbers of fish in a water and it is easy to imagine that huge waters contain vast numbers of fish. The fish finder proves that this is not always the case and that stocks can be very concentrated at specific times of the year. So it is probably with these spawning char gathered together from all over the loch system and, for a while, very vulnerable to angling pressure. For this reason, it is a great shame that so many are killed – largely by game anglers from both north and south of the border. To the majority of these men, catch and release is a foreign concept. From childhood they have been brought up to kill what they catch for the pot. A coarse fisherman is naturally brought up differently and I have caught and released and re-caught char which have suffered no apparent damage. Game anglers have things to teach coarse men, it's true, but in this respect, at least, coarse must come in the future to educate game.

2

Irish Adventure

A Month in Ireland

In December 1989, a float went down at the Flyfisher's Lake in Norfolk and a 39½lb pike was landed. For everyone gathered around, this was an awe-inspiring moment. Miller, Jim Tyree, Dave Plummer, Ritchie Furlong, myself and the rest of us had all seen 30lb pike but this fish was special because of more than its size alone: its colours shone so brilliantly, it was as if there were a glow around the fish, a radiating force of anger and barely subdued power. I look back now on the photographs of that fish and I see both Miller and me drenched, stunned, barely able to support or to take in the enormity of the fish on our laps. That pike was staggering and that night I drove away from the Flyfisher's Lake with my mind in turmoil. I knew two things: this giant pike was *the* one that Miller and I had planned for and fished for for so long; and that furthermore we would be lucky to better it – ever – from the waters of East Anglia. I knew that I would pike fish in Norfolk in the future but I also realized that for my dream pike I had to make fresh beginnings.

Of course, Scottish pike have always enthralled me, in Loch Lomond especially. We know that Tommy Morgan caught a 47-pounder there and Fred Buller lost one of the same ilk, and I believe that there are one or two fish of this calibre alive there today. Yes, I accept the salmon runs are not what they were and the powan shoals are probably reduced. I agree that most big females would head for the well-known, heavily fished spawning beds and a monster should therefore have been caught or at least sighted in the last few years. Certainly, it does seem that big Lomond pike level out at 30 to 34lb and even a very large 30-pounder would be an event. But all this does not mean that a super pike does not exist, unguessed-at, out in the loch. Perhaps she keeps deep and does not spawn, at least with the general run of fish.

My knowledge of more northerly lochs is greater than it is of Loch

[48]

One of my Flyfisher's Lake fish.

The winter of 1989, Dave Plummer and Kevin Grix enjoy breakfast at the Flyfisher's Lake.

Dave Plummer with a typical trout lake '20'.

The 39½lb Flyfisher's Lake monster. What could remain after this?

Lomond and my experience seems to suggest that the vast majority of pike are jacks with just a few doubles creeping to around 20lb. It would be easy to write off waters like this, but out of the deep blue depths, just once a decade, comes a massive fish. Sometimes it is landed. More often it is lost by a Scottish trout fisher just filling in a boring winter Sunday and quite unprepared for a leviathan. This is not speculation; I know it to be true. I have seen one carcase, three photographs, a bow wave; I have spoken to witnesses and seen one spectacular fight end in favour of a never remotely beaten fish. What I do repeat, though, is that Scottish super-pike are very, very few. Perhaps each loch holds just one for a few years out of each twenty. It could be anywhere in miles of near bottomless water and it probably feeds irregularly on a salmon, a large trout, or from a single lunge into a shoal of char sixty feet below the surface. There are also the jacks to contend with. Any run in Scotland can be an event but for it then to be a 2-pounder is a bitter blow, out there in the wind and rain. I witnessed 150 anglers fish a pike match on one of the 'better' lochs. Through a long day only three pike, totalling 16lb, were landed. A one thousand to one chance said that a single fish could have weighed 40lb at least. Such is Scottish piking.

A mean Scottish double wins the pike match.

The great Buller pike looks on.

Ireland, though, I knew to be different. Through story, legend and Fred Buller's *Domesday Book of Pike*, (Stanley Paul, 1979). It was Fred I contacted and it was through Fred that I managed to secure a long stay in the west of Ireland, within casting range of those very waters that had between them produced half a century of 35lb-plus pike. So it was I found myself before a great peat fire in a totally isolated white-washed cottage, tucked away in County Mayo, while the wind beat away outside. Above me, as a spur, hung the great man's great pike itself – 32lb of menace, flickering through the firelight.

The first morning of my stay, I took a boat from the side of the house and I put it on Lough Mask. Till dusk I motored around the shore of this vast lake, not daring to go further out than a mile or so, looking almost with fear over the inland ocean still churning ahead of me. The second dawn I put the second boat on Corrib and spent two days on a water I had never seen the like of before. I was entranced by the sudden lights of sunshine that came from a cloud-ridged sky. The lake, I knew, had been created by an angler god: a shoreline pock-marked with bays, a rash of islands, spits, arms, reefs, drop-offs. I realized in those two days that with Mask and Corrib I faced an unknowable idyll. No life would be long enough to know waters as vast as these; whatever size fish you caught, you would never know if it was the ultimate monster of the deeps.

A Mask pike in a period of calm.

Neville Fickling and Des Elliott meet on Mask.

Even a fool can see at once why Mask and Corrib have produced so many big pike. They are simply the Flyfisher's Lake magnified thousands of times. They are vast, clear, salmonoid-rich waters where the pike stocks are continually culled by gill nets and Irish anglers. Those pike that do escape persecution have every opportunity to become huge. Within the week I had spoken to a man who had claimed a 56¼lb pike, taken from him by a Frenchman and to a second man who possessed the head of a pike which had been killed by an otter and which had weighed 56lb with several chunks missing! And so it went on. Though I half disbelieved them I could not doubt the monsters that I saw cased in bars, hotels and fishery huts around the loughs. There was a white cottage for sale, as regular as a child's drawing, with a path leading straight to its own beach and boat on Corrib. I could live there, piking all day every day, learn, and finally catch pike to dwarf that giant from the Flyfisher's Lake. I did not have the money but the dream is still there.

Certainly, my performance that month needed improving upon. While I clicked at once with the big wild brown trout, pike frustrated me throughout. The main water bodies on the loughs were too vast for my boat to make any impression upon, especially during a continually rough period of gales and storms. I was forced into the bays which I found nigh on impossible to troll deeply and slowly. The depths there were chaotic;

Hardly an Irish bar without its giant pike.

weed, sunken timber and hedgerows seemed ever present. I was forced to fish bait – dead sea fish, trout and perch – and on gin–clear trout waters I would have been far happier with the livebaits, outlawed by the Irish.

My confidence picked up one day of constant storm which Des, Joy and I still tried to troll through. There behind a Mask island, lay anchored the boat of Neville Fickling. Simply by fishing deads in the lee of islands that day he had picked up three fine fish to 16lb. He knew, I knew and all of you will know, that any one of those could have been a monster.

By the end of my Irish time, I had formulated a plan: we would go back on to Corrib with two boats for the whole of the spring. We would fish bay after bay from dawn to dusk without a break. We could festoon the area with deadbaits and we would troll. We would sleep in local bed and breakfast or inns and keep on the move until we located big fish, which we must eventually do by this method. The problems would be immense I knew – time, expense, maintenance of two boats, two engines and two sets of gear, limitations on methods, the inevitable severe weather – but we would continue on undaunted until success came our way. Who knows, by the time this book is published we might just have done it.

Des introduces himself as a ferox master!

Irish Ferox

Of course, I did not travel to Ireland for pike alone. Long ago, stories of big ferox taken by Fred Wagstaffe to 13lb, by Bill Keale to 16lb and more recently a fish of 17lb landed by Dubliner Des Elliot made me keen to bring my Scottish experience to bear. I was fortunate to meet Des very early on in my stay and it was a magical introduction. He had been out very early in the morning and he called round to the cottage for a coffee and to show the catch. The largest trout was a shadow under double figures. Des is a gentle, softly spoken Irish man who spends every free moment on the western lochs. We settled down, happy to talk big trout. I described the fishing in Scotland and he pointed me to the bays in the islands that he believed would do me proud during my stay – if I could ride the winds to reach them. As the days progressed, we met often, in the same boat or on the same water, or simply passing by in the lanes to secluded harbourages around the loughs. One day he told me he believed the wind was gentle enough – just – for me to make a troll around Devenish Island. The legend of this big island mid-way out in Mask is immense and as I set out I could just see it, riding the waves far out. In an hour, I was there.

The wind was coming from the west and the east shore was well sheltered and reached depths of twenty to forty feet. The Humminbird showed plenty of fish and I trolled the half-mile island up and down twice

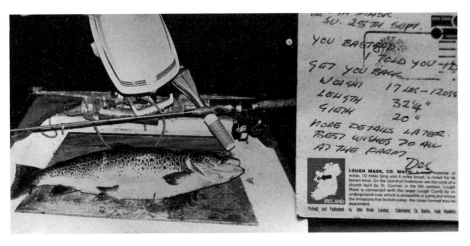

Des Elliott's monster and postcard to Fred Buller.

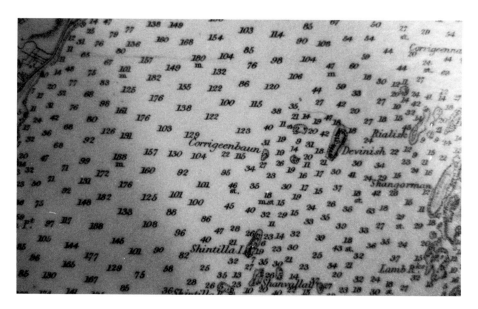

An old Admiralty chart of Lough Mask.

for a brown of some 3lb. Now, whether I liked it or not, I had to brave the windward shore, the famous one, the bank of big fish in the past.

Trolling up the island, I was struck by the full force of the gusts and fought to keep the boat and two rods working. The picture I got over the Humminbird's screen was a dramatic one. The depth changes were continuous with sharp drop-offs and deep water close in to the rocks where the water foamed. There were also the images of good fish lying around the twenty-foot contour.

Half-way up on the first troll, I had a savage take and knew at once the fish was big. It came in towards the boat deep and then simply stuck at around twenty-five feet. Nothing I could do would lift it and, at last, one of its dogged, boring runs saw the hook shake free. I very nearly wept.

Towards the end of that first pass up wind off Devinish, I hooked a small trout that I tried to skip in around the other trailing line. I failed and the knitted lines tied me, boat, engine and my 1lb fish like a parcel. All I could do was to drift in confusion to a sheltered beach, clear everything up and start again. I knew, though, that all of this would be a struggle. The wind has risen again and the constant storm-tossing had led to a headache and then to growing nausea in the pit of my stomach. I was also sick at heart over the loss of such a fish, a beauty never even seen.

Strangely, the sun, that long-distant friend, came out over the cloud bars, and insects at once rose off the calm water at the toe of the island. A trout rolled lazily and the spreading ripples washed at the boat. I knew that I would go to Devenish again.

Even more strangely, at exactly the same point in the troll, the rod went round again and another big fish was on. This one too came in deep and stayed there, plugging remorsely for fifteen minutes while I drifted along in the wind. It was the very twin of the last fish and I was on my knees in the boat well, in fight . . . in prayer . . .

The fish began to rise. It leapt four feet out of the water. As it leapt it caught the sun and I marvelled at it as a primitive man at a shooting star. 'Thwack' it fell and the fight was gone out of us both. I netted it and made for the bank and back to the island retreat I had left only thirty minutes before. 9lb and a bit. Now, I was singing.

Thanks to Fred and thanks to Des, that whole month was kind to me. I had some forty fish over 4lb by the end of the stay. I felt I had taken enough trout to learn lessons and even to develop ideas that could work for me in the Highlands when I returned there.

The lures that did best for me were large, silver and brass spoons, brightly polished with a single well-sharpened treble. A good bold action that got the rod tip bouncing increased my confidence and perhaps, as a result, the number of takes too. Two traces and two swivels did a great deal to prevent that troller's curse, line twist, that can become a nightmare after a long day on the water with spinners.

Trolling speed was vital. I found I could move the boat quite fast and the hits were nearly all converted to hooked fish. Slow the boat down and the number of knocks grew and true rod-benders fell. At times I was going quite half throttle, even with the wave behind me. A variation of speed and course often converted a following, tapping trout into a well-hooked one, as did quite violent up and down, backward and forward motions on the rod. I became firmly convinced that these big browns were often not taking the lures instantly but rather following for fifty or even a hundred yards and that they often needed to be agitated into a full-blooded strike.

The Irish venture proved an important first indication to me that not all ferox are to be caught deep down. At the speed I was trolling, with few or no leads on the line, it is doubtful whether my spoons were working at more than ten feet but the big trout came up in numbers. This I was to remember in Scotland and to act upon.

Gales and the hazardous nature of Mask and Corrib taught me to hone my boat drill quickly. It was either learn or die. Presuming I was alone,

Ferox fishing in a frame.

A finely marked ferox.

once the trout was on, I slipped the engine into neutral and never off. Then I reeled in the second rod to avoid the otherwise inevitable tangle of crossed lines. Not once did the hooked trout escape in this thirty-second manoeuvre. I could then play the fish with a clear field, though keeping a constant eye on the drift of the boat. Barely submerged rocks and reefs riddled both loughs and could prove lethal. For this reason, it was vital not to let the engine die during the fight – you simply cannot play a big fish and start up the engine. Almost inevitably in these heavy swells, I played the fish on my knees, safe on the boards of the boat. The net would be set up and naturally I would lean as little as possible over the side when the end of the battle came.

The Boat Strike

The Irish boat strike of the late 1980s is now legendary. The two years of strife between the boating and fishing community and the Government could almost be described as a civil war and I was one of the first anglers visiting since late 1987. The Irish people showed extraordinary resilience to the Government's attempt to impose a rod licence. Over and over the reasons were explained to me precisely. Firstly, if the Government

A fine Mask trout .

imposed a licence it presumed that the fishing rights were not commonly held and free but that the angler was in fact a licensee. This concept went quite against what the Irish people themselves believed. Secondly, as a licensee, the angler would be subject to Government controls and rules. The waters would no longer be controlled by the men actually fishing them. Thirdly, as a licensor, the Government would be able to grant use of the lochs to other interests as well as to angling and the one interest that the Irish suspected more than any was the fish farming interest. The strength of the boat strike on Mask and Corrib should guarantee that no concern will ever dare to despoil the loughs as they have done the lochs! All the suffering that these people underwent for two years would oblige the sinking of any cage that should appear in the future. The two years of fighting was worth it to save what is a near perfect environment and how brave of the Irish around the shores of these great loughs to sacrifice a good deal of daily bread to repulse the encroachments of commercialism.

Resistance was very strong all over Ireland, but the hotbed was found on the shores of Mask and Corrib, centering perhaps, on the village of Cong. Here, opposition to the licence was immense. No local wanted to go out and even though the boatman had said that the old and the young would not be harassed, they desisted from fishing. Pitiful it was, people say, to see the old people watching the lakes, longing to be on them,

Rare Irish calm and a typical Mask trout.

wondering if their time would come before the end of the strike, but supporting it one and all, none the less. For one old man at least, the solution came too late. For the last two seasons of his life he had merely watched the water and walked the shore and he died the winter before the final settlement.

A few men from afar dared to go on and had their boats holed, their engines destroyed and were threatened in the bars. There were demonstrations, 'fish-ins' without a licence, organized by the locals. All of these were quelled by the authorities. One of them at Cong backfired miserably on the police force. Three unlicensed anglers were arrested: a young mother of three, the nineteen-year-old son of a widow and the wife of a helpless, paralysed man. These three 'desperadoes' were taken nearly as far as Dublin before the authorities realized how foolish they were looking. Their fine was paid for them, they were given lunch and a free taxi ride back home from the Irish Midlands!

Forms of Suicide

Of all the skills a ferox or big-water pikeman needs, near-perfect boat control is the prime one. Obviously, this comes from practice in the main but there are certain guide-lines to follow. *In Wild Waters* merely covered the basics: a stable boat, a reliable engine, sufficient petrol reserves, rowlocks, life-jackets and bailing buckets were all deemed necessities. Since then, Stephen Harper has brought out *Angling Afloat* (The Crowood Press, 1989) and the chapters by Neville Fickling and Gord Burton especially, make valuable reading. Both, however, miss saying that in very wild weather it is still possible to fish with the wind, complete a troll and then motor back against the wind with no lines out. If the wind is very high and your troll down with it is too fast, your boat can be slowed down by using a drogue over the stern.

There are occasions, though, when fate takes its toll and when even to think of going afloat is, in truth, a form of suicide.

3.35 p.m., and I have had to stop trolling, pull off the arm of Mask and sit the day away in a backwater. The wind, which was force 5, is now gusting force 8 or perhaps even 9. A farmer even called to me a few minutes ago to come in. 'Storms, terrible storms,' he shouted. 'Give it up boy, now, when you have got a chance.' Quite gladly, I consented. I knew that I should never really have started out in the first place.

Wild Irish days; Des Elliott claps and Joy hopes for life.

At 8.30 a.m. – beyond the spit that separated me from Mask – the wind was piling up the rollers, drenching the shoreline with spray. But I had found two new bays and could not ignore them. Also the frustration of being kept in the house was in me like the damp, like rot, like blight. Go out on to Mask I must.

I took what precautions I could, an extra can of fuel, a spare oar, my life-jacket zipped as well as tied and even a silent prayer said as I slipped down the arm towards the first bay. It was there the wind hit me, rolling down from the north-west, from around the peak of Mauntrasna and giving a wave of two feet. Still I braved it. Trolling was possible with a single rod and the engine at three-quarter throttle. I was glad that I faced it all. By 2 p.m. I had taken seven trout to an ounce under 5lb with several around 3lb and a beautiful perch of $1\frac{1}{2}$lb. I took lunch hurriedly for I more than half expected something sensational in that killing period between 3 p.m. and 5 p.m. I got more than I ever bargained for. There was no doubt about it, the wind was up a notch or two. The whole Partry range of mountains was bathed in mist, and now rain, then sleet, lashed the lake. Keeping the boat on anything like a course was a nightmare but still, as I chugged up the bay, I had another take which urged me on. Each wave now was white capped and each sweep of wind juddered the boat beyond

A fine Mask perch.

endurance. A particularly ferocious squall swept my fuel funnel over-board. This was a disaster. I was burning petrol prodigiously and to refill on such a sea without a funnel would have been hopeless. The funnel was floating, however, and I wound in the spoon, throttled the boat into the wave and around after it. The boat bucked and dropped and twisted and the engine came off, lashing angrily in the foam, held on only by the cord. I wrestled to hold it out of the water, managed to switch it off and pulled it to the side of the boat. A wave threw me on my back but I dared not let go of my hold. A second wave dashed the engine against the transom, crushing my finger and making it bleed over the boards. Finally the engine was in. Time was tight, as the swell was piling me in towards the rocks. With only yards to spare, the boat wheeled away again, safe into deep water, with the deck a maelstrom of tackle, blood and the three kept fish.

Sanctuary was essential and a hundred yards off to my left it appeared in the form of a cove sheltered by steep rock on the fringe of a forest. Inside its mouth, the water was narrow but deep and, above all, calm. Hardly had I entered than the engine faltered and ran completely out of fuel. Here was peace from the wind, the rain and the 4 horsepower growl! I lay in the well of the boat and laughed, watching the delicate birch and alders slide

The pike, the hook, and the finger.

by above me. Quite quickly. Faster. I sensed alarm and struggled to my knees. The cove was nothing but the neck of a river which thundered angrily towards a gorge twenty yards away from me. If I went into that I would be swallowed and swept underground for miles before being belched out into Lough Corrib. The engine was useless. The oars were not in position and only the third one was accessible. I rammed it down ahead of me and mercifully I found bottom. Bit by bit I poled myself back up the cove to a tiny bay where I beached, tied up and collapsed well and truly into the soaked grasses. I was refitted and refuelled when I heard the call and saw the farmer wave. It was 3.20 p.m. or thereabouts then and I knew that I had had enough. My crushed finger, numb back and beating heart all told me so.

There were other dangers. I had been frustrated by the number of false knocks to my big spinners and I began to experiment with outrider hooks and hooks drilled into the top of the spoon that would attach a fish trying to take it head first. The improvement was only marginal but I stuck with the concept until one particular day. Again, Mask was the scene. It was 9 a.m. on another windy, grey, damp day. I had been out since 7 and at 8.30 had taken a 10lb hen pike. I worked that troll a second time and almost at once

I was into a jack. I got it on board and prepared to take out the hooks. The jack wriggled and leapt. I lost hold. He dropped and in so doing, pulled the top treble into my index finger, well past the barb. For thirty seconds I panicked. Each time the pike leapt it pulled my agonized finger after it. The engine had stalled and I was going out of control, very quickly, on to a series of jagged rocks. I had a choice. I could have lain in the boat and waited for death. I had to do something. I decided to act. The first need was to detach myself from that pike, and fast. Needs must and I killed it – with difficulty as my right hand had to follow the fish with every blow which my left hand gave its skull against the oar. Then I had to lever the treble and my finger from the split ring. Blood, rain, nausea, giddiness and a layer of slime everywhere made the job hard going but finally the hook came off. I lurched to the engine and from the teeth of the rocks I pulled the boat away.

I sat on an island and fiddled miserably with forceps. Though I could bend the shank the hook would still not come free. The pain was now diabolical and I took the boat back to Cush Lough, feeling as dead as the jack that stared at me coldly from the planks. A bad day for us both I felt. I asked at the farm for a doctor. 'Be Jesus' was all I got. Ballinrobe was wet and half shut down for St Patrick's Day celebrations. The surgery was obviously in the closed half. I rang a number and was told to wait a half-hour. I wandered to the pub where my plight was soon noticed. Amputation! Gangrene! A knife job for sure! Gas? At least another hundred remarks helped a whiskey or two down. Fortified, but not optimistic, I wandered to the surgery. The doctor, bless him, only seemed interested in the hook make! A push, a wriggle, a surge of pain and the barb was proud of the flesh. A snip and I was free and within an hour I was back on Lough Mask.

The Dream

The day, as usual, had been foul and we had been so wet and wind-tossed that there was no desire left in us to go out into the town bars that night. Baked potatoes and fresh Mask trout eaten, a whiskey or two taken in front of Fred's enormous fire and it was time to climb the stairs and settle into the bedclothes, enveloped for warmth against the gale around the gables. Sleep was instant and dreams seemed constant. One was remembered in the grey dawn. It was evening in high summer, on a lake small by Mask standards. My old angling chum, Joe Reed, stood to my

The splendour of Mask.

left, Fred Buller himself to my right then Richard Walker and last in the line Fred J. Taylor. In the very clear water I could see tench browsing and turning all through the golden sunset. The light faded and we all prepared to sleep out the night ready for the dawn session. Joe and I shared an umbrella. The other three sat on the ground, played cards and finally slept on the hard earth.

Out of the half light, there came a smell of cooking. Fred J. T. crouched over a fire where bacon sizzled. A bird or two was singing and Walker was swearing at everyone to wake up in a rough country dialect. Buller prepared the swims but no one was allowed to fish until breakfast was taken, enjoyed and complimented upon. Joe and I could soon see that the tench were finicky. We had them feeding but no bites were forthcoming though we could hear splashing from all the neighbouring swims. We tipped each other a wink, reeled in, put hairs on our hooks and baited delicately with a couple of maggots. We had more action but the hairs were constantly bitten off, the bites remained fiddly and we were driven half mad for a couple of small tench.

The sun was high and we all packed up. Between them, Buller, Taylor and Walker were putting back over two dozen fish. Walker laughed out

[69]

A dark castle and Corrib's shining water.

The starving look on.

loud at us. 'Keep the bait half an inch off the bottom when they are finicky,' he said. 'An exact half an inch. An old trick. Hair rigs! Freds, hear that? Oh my! Lads today!'

Tales of the Islands

I heard something of my old heroes, men who had gone to the big loughs a quarter of a century ago, lived rough on the islands and had trolled for the big trout. They had all received great help and kindness from the Irish people; yet a few of those around them once slipped off the lough early in the morning, unscrewed several Irish engines and loaded them into their vehicle. These engines were then sold to pay for the trip and the genuine English anglers unfortunately found the Irish less willing to open their arms to them in the future. The islands themselves are strange places. Some of them are straddled by old fortifications, often eleventh-century, built by English or Irish chieftains as handy escape holes from wandering raiding parties. Most of the bigger islands are the home of goats, rowed out there by land-hungry farmers and turned loose to fend for themselves. They are virtually wild now and watch suspiciously from the under-growth as you troll past. Sadly, in the winter, there is not enough food to keep the population alive and come the spring, you find the new flowers bursting into bloom around the rotting corpses of the poor starved animals.

3

The Wild Carp Trail

The Boathouse Lake Wild Carp

The Boathouse Lake was central, in the book *In Wild Waters*, as the home of large, long-lived mirror carp. For a couple of years I was obsessed with the place but what I did not mention in that earlier book was that the lake possessed wild carp. They, in fact, had been the focus of my original interest in the water many years before I was aware of the scope of the mirror carp. During the later 1980s my fascination with the mirror carp had tended to make me lose interest somewhat in the wild carp population and it was only by 1988 that I realized that the lake now held very few of these once-prolific fish. In 1989 I again visited the water for a four-day session. The weather was invariably hot, settled and bright. Norfolk was in the middle of a drought and the water was very low and very clear; I felt at many times I could see virtually most of the fish in the lake. I recognized many of the mirrors that I had caught and the occasional one that I had not. I studied the bream shoal and could even count the individual members of it. I was also very much aware that wild carp were now few in number. One particular fish struck me by its agitated and eccentric behaviour. Most mornings it swam around the boathouse in a peculiar gyrating fashion and I began to wonder if all was well with it.

The fishing during that spell was very difficult indeed. The carp that I found bolted, even from the sight of the line in the water. I found it was imperative that this lay well hidden along the bottom in weed patches, or even in the end, around the fringes of islands. The mirrors were hypersensitive to my presence and I spent most of the time well hidden behind trees or anything up to fifteen yards away from the water's edge. I continued to see the distressed wild carp during all this time and one afternoon it appeared on the surface and seemed to me to be taking food there.

Over the years it had been rare for a Boathouse Lake carp to take a

A tremor down the flank caused me to rejoice and think the fish was alive again.

floating bait but on this particular occasion I decided to try it. I put on a simple piece of crust and cast it out into the vicinity of the rising wild carp. A long while passed and quite unexpectedly a dark form came to the bread, sucked it in and was away down the lake. I struck and for three or four minutes enjoyed a spectacular fight. Indeed, for a very short while, by the power of that fish, I was convinced that I had at least a 20lb mirror on line. Quickly, however, I saw that the culprit was the wild carp that I had planned for and eventually he began to roll in a tired fashion in front of the net. Two yards out everything simply stopped. It was as though the fish had thrown the hook and I was reeling in an inert clump of weed. No, it was the fish. I netted it and it did not move. I took the hook out and it simply lay there. I could not understand this but as I held it for a photograph I thought it was beginning to wriggle. I was wrong. I put the fish back in the water and it simply floated – quite, quite dead. I was absolutely horrified. The death of my first big ferox still hung heavily upon me and now the stress of battle had caused this find old wild carp to die also. I was utterly woebegone.

I spent ages, crouched there in the heat, trying to work some life back into the fish. It was of no use and I was forced to accept that the fish had died of stress or a heart attack. I took the body into the wood, dug a shallow grave and buried him on the banks of his long-loved home water.

[73]

A tragedy . . . the Boathouse Lake fish in death.

This was enough for me that day and I drove home, quietly reflective.

That night I met Miller in the pub and we talked about the dead fish. He was quite adamant that I should not have buried the fish at all but, seeing as it had died on me in such a tragic fashion, I should rather have had it set up for historic and sentimental reasons. I realized that he was correct and left the house at 2 a.m. to be at the lake well before first light. As the first rays of dawn crept over the water I made my way into the wood and followed my footsteps to where the fish was buried. The grave had been rudely disturbed and the carcass of the fish lay before me at least a quarter eaten by either fox or badger. I had truly wasted the life of this fine fish.

Some days later I received back the photographs of the capture and looked at them with interest. I am smiling as I hold the fish because I mistakenly felt the pulse of life and believed that the wild carp had in actual fact woken up again. However, it was the fish itself that fascinated me. Surely, the body was a little too deep and a little too rounded to be a true wild carp. I also looked closely at its mouth and saw little sign of any noticeable barbules. I began to wonder if my wildie was a true specimen at all. That it was magnificent, I had no doubt, but was it really a hybrid or even some strain of carp now extinct! The body, sadly, would be of little use now to science and it was only possible to hypothesize. Later that day I caught one of my big mirrors and I left the lake there and then for good.

I felt it had given me all I could ever want from it and to continue would have been selfish and uncaring.

For the next few weeks I addressed myself to the state of wild carp in Norfolk. The more I travelled and the more I saw, the more I realized that wild carp populations in Norfolk are fast disappearing. In the 1960s the county had been the bastion of wild carp but now everthing seemed to be crumbling around them. Here, disease had wiped out the population. There, a pond had been drained and was even built upon. In other waters the introduction of mirror and king and common carp had obviously tampered with the old genetic wild strain. In short, I could now only find a handful of waters which I could trust to produce the genuine wild carp article. Now my interest in wild carp was thoroughly aroused and it was to be increased by an article I was to read and by letters to Alwyne Wheeler, the great fish expert of this country.

Wildies, Science and History

Shortly after the death of the Boathouse Lake wild carp I picked up a copy of *Coarse Angler* magazine and read the following article by Chris Currie. I was totally fascinated and am delighted to publish it here, where it belongs as one of the motivating forces in the quest that was to follow.

Wild Carp Now an Endangered Species?

Chris Currie

During archaeological excavations at Castle Bromwich Hall Gardens, West Midlands, under my direction, a small, early eighteenth century formal pond was discovered at the end of the western vista through the ten-acre, walled garden. This pond was in a remarkably fine state of preservation, which enabled us as archaeologists to come to a number of interesting conclusions about the pond-makers' lost art.

The pond appeared to have been built around 1730 and to have been filled in before 1802 at the latest. As a result, more recent changes, so often the bane of archaeologists working on old ponds, simply had not occurred. The clay walls, the pond lining and its brick and sandstone sluice were all perfectly preserved. The latter was the first example to have been discovered of a type of sluice later used by Lancelot 'Capability' Brown, and works on a principle similar to the presently popular 'Monk'.

Considering the rarity of such undisturbed period pieces, the Garden's Committee, which oversees the technical work of restoration, recommended restoring the pond to its original condition. Earlier work in the gardens had already reinstated a rectangular pond 28.5 × 15m, (31 × 16yd) and after some deliberation it was decided to stock both ponds with carp, as these were considered the most fitting eighteenth century species. On my advice the gardens decided that the introduced fish must be wild, scaled carp and not the more recently introduced mirror carp. However obtaining wild fish proved to be more of a problem than anticipated, and resulted in my decision to write this article.

I contacted Keith Easton of Severn-Trent Water Authority, an authority on the history of carp, hoping to obtain some unwanted 'wildies' through him. I was surprised to learn that the true wild strain was nearing extinction, because the boom in stocking with mirrors and other 'king' carp has contaminated the gene pool to such an extent that there are now very few places in the UK where wild fish can be found.

This particularly surprised me because I have spent some time over the last 24 years fishing for wild carp, and have had them up to $15\frac{1}{2}$lb in weight. On talking to Keith I discovered that even in the Danube, the now archaeologically proven homeland of all European carp, the wildie population, once so numerous, has been so infiltrated by king carp that the strain is no longer pure.

Keith told me that only fish that had never been in contact with king carp can be genuinely called wildies. Once just one king carp is introduced, such a fish will add its genes to the spawn pool every spring to the extent that no subsequently bred fish can be given the name wildie, regardless of its shape. Although I have always accepted this principle, it was only when I thought hard about it that I realised how quickly the process has been irreversibly enacted.

My own experience confirms this as all the waters where I have fished for wild carp have either been filled in, netted and restocked, turned into trout fisheries, or have had king carp introduced to them.

Highbridge gravel pits and Rooksbury Park in Hampshire, were both once prolific wildie pools, but both have had small numbers of king carp introduced. Although, in the case of Highbridge, only about four fish were added to the wildie population, this is sufficient to put the parentage of any fish from that water in doubt. There were a number of other small pits at Highbridge that never received extra fish but these have now either been filled or they dried up in the drought of 1976.

All the other wildie pools where I have fished have now gone in the ways described above. Most of the more substantial waters have now been restocked with king carp. It is only when the situation is viewed nation-wide that the extent of the 'damage' is perceived. I enclose the 'damage' in quotations because, as an angler, I have often whole-heartedly supported such moves. It wasn't until I tried to get hold of the once-common wildie that I realized what has happened.

So, a problem exists for the wild carp. The authorities are unlikely to recognize that the wildie has become an endangered species as a carp, *Cyprinus carpio*, is a carp to them. From the angling point of view I doubt if anyone will bemoan the change from wildies to the larger king carp. Only real purists will miss the wildie and those, like myself, who have been privileged to fish those rare waters where only a few fish were stocked and they somehow failed to breed prolifically. On such occasions, fish to 15lb and possibly larger could have been encountered. When such fishing can be found it is superior to that obtainable from king carp, as I can testify.

One category of citizen will miss the wildie. It is people, like myself, who are involved in the restoration of old ponds, either as part of an overall historic garden design, or in their own right. This practice is becoming increasingly popular at the moment and if historic interpretation is to be correct, the correct fish should be put in, otherwise I feel something is lost. There is nothing worse than visiting an historic garden or parkland site that is described as 'authentically' restored to its original period, and to find kois or goldfish swimming around in the ponds! Somehow I find that a bit of an insult.

Personally I would like to see certain existing wildie pools protected, but I somehow doubt the practicalities of such efforts. Sooner or later the 'big is best' mentality would prevail and mirrors would get in, either legally, through administrative ignorance on the part of the controlling body, or illegally through the efforts of local carp anglers who will think they are secretly doing everyone a favour. At present it has been decided to set Castle Bromwich Hall Gardens up as a breeding site for wild carp. At least then one small site can be relied on to supply the fish to those requiring 'authentic' carp to inhabit their restored historic ponds.

After reading this piece, I thought very hard about a lake I had heard of in Wales. Rumour had it to be over a thousand years old and stocked with carp by monks in medieval times. Since then, there had been no further stocking, people assured me and, if carp did still exist there, I felt that they must be true wild carp. I wrote to that great fish expert, Alwyne Wheeler for his opinion and here publish his reply.

Dear John

There are no real differences between wild carp and common carp in terms of scale or fin ray counts and taxonomists recognise them both as a simple species, *Cyprinus carpio*. But

Wildie or common? A fine fish in any event.

there is a difference in body form. The wild carp is slender, flat bellied and with only a gently curved back and looks very athletic compared to the common carp. (It is a bit like comparing Sebastian Coe with a Sumo wrestler!)

However, I do not think that there are any wild carp in Britain, even ones from the tidal Thames have that deep body and swollen appearance (although not so grotesque as many still water carp), and I suspect that this is because they were introduced as cultivated fish.

To see real wild carp you have to fish in places like Lake Volvi (Macedonia) or in the Danube. In both, the carp caught are slender-bodied and greyhounds compared with most of our carp. In Lake Volvi they are fished for commercially using long-lines and a gorge (baited with sweetcorn!), and this is one of the few natural native populations left in Europe. Elsewhere the preponderance of cultivated, fast-growing, fat fish is such that the genuine wild European fish is in danger of disappearing.

I hope this rambling letter helps.

Best wishes,

Alwyne Wheeler

Welsh Adventure

Alwyne Wheeler's letter inspired me. Of course, I knew that I would have to go to this cradle of carp and investigate the birthplace of true wild fish. But first there was something else I wanted to try. My Wye adventures had led me deep into Wales where I had heard a lot about carp fishing. I realized that, as far as wild carp went, parts of Wales were probably in the same state as Norfolk had been quarter of a century ago. Tucked away in valleys were almost forgotten waters, untampered with, where carp had remained genetically sound for countless generations. Peter Smith was my contact, the owner of Cae'r Beris Manor Hotel – one of the finest anglers' hostels imaginable. I sent him a letter. I received a phone call and I was with him in Wales just before the season's end.

He sent me first to a lake we will call Black Hound's Tarn. There were elements of insanity about that trip. It was late February and the water was situated on a plateau of moorland just under 1,500 feet high – not ideal carping altitudes, one would have thought. However, there had been week upon week of warm, wet westerlies without any sign of a frost. The lake had risen and been stirred around by the wind and rain and it all seemed quite possible. Carp had been there for generations and Peter told me it had been a stewpond for a brotherhood of Cistercian monks situated on the bleak moors. If this was all true then the carp should have become hardy to an extreme degree and would not be put off feeding during the

Sunset over a Welsh wildie lake.

winter months. And, after all, the month was so mild that it could have been taken for April or later. There was frog-spawn around and the new nettles were growing well. I discovered that the lake was very shallow and still heavily weeded from the previous year. Indeed, the water is, apparently, choked with weed come the summer when it is impossible to force a bait into the water anywhere. All this made more sense of my decision to fish when I did.

You might wonder about the name of the lake. The story is well known around this part of Wales that the moor was the inspiration for Conan Doyle's story *The Hound of the Baskervilles*. A great sheep-eating dog had long been at large on the hills and it must have been easy to imagine Watson and Holmes striding the bleak landscape. The setting of the tale was moved to south-west England only to save the embarrassment of the local gentry, those famous Baskervilles whose name still swings above the door of the local pub.

The whole story smacks of Gothic horrors. On my first day I simply walked to find the water and put in bait. The evening was spent around a log fire in the hotel and the night in a lofty bedroom overlooking the river gorge. About 2 a.m. I was awoken by a flash of light around the room and instantly a tremendous thunderclap followed. There were three such and

February and carping at 1,500 feet.

Typical ferox country cloaked in autumn's colours.

A magnificent ferox weighing in at slightly under 13lb.

Three char totalling over 12lb, all tragically killed as they approached their spawning season.

A fine wildie from one of the oldest lakes in Wales.

A large barbel runs for freedom in a central European river.

An unusually hump-backed fish for the Balkans.

The classic wildie: bullet-shaped and subdued in colour.

Nase profile: a very lovely fish with the mouth of a mullet.

In these large European backwaters huge catfish, carp and pike live the summer out.

John Bailey and Paul Boote are objects of fascination in the crowded Dehra Dun bazaar.

*A first sight of the Ganges, roaring, swollen, hundreds of feet
beneath the camera crew.*

Under the lens of John 'the Cam', Paul Boote plays a Ganges monster.

One of the beautiful carp-rich Kashmir lakes.

then hail beat against the mullioned windows. After a quarter of an hour the night was gentle once more.

Next day I fished from dawn to dusk in as wild a water as I have ever known. I never saw another soul nor heard any sound but the continuous rush of wind, frequent splattering of rain on my hood and the occasional mewings from the buzzards when the sun broke through. A driving gale never let up and as blue sky displaced the cloud, constant rainbows shimmered above the water. My baits, though, lay untouched and I walked the hills that circled the pool. From up high, when the sun burst through, the weed was clear to see. I went back to the gear, and increased the length of tail, still trusting that there were fish to see the bait. The day was short and the sun was visibly dropping in the sky. The cloud had gone and now a chill descended. The wind at last began to drop and the lake to settle a little. Everything was bathed in lights of blue and gold. Just once then, a long way out, a fish jumped. I couldn't see whether or not it was a carp, big or small, but it cheered me to see the lake alive a little. Encouraged, I stayed on until the light turned and the chill grew intense. Then I remembered the last words spoken in the bar the previous night. 'Of course, there's them that say there is still animals up there you wouldn't want to meet at night!' I remembered the catalogue of sheep throats torn out, of deer hauled down in fright and I shuffled away, a solitary figure, off the moor.

The bar was another warm, light world. I ordered a drink and the old boys took it upon themselves to talk in their own dear Welsh. I enjoyed the lilt and the strangeness and then the novelty of a voice in English. 'Did you hear about God talking to Archangel Gabriel, explaining like how he built the world?'

"Well," he said, "I gave each country some good and some bad – like Egypt. A lot of desert, but lush, fertile oases. Or Norway with sheltered fjords but a bleak inland."

"But what of Wales?" asked Gabriel. "That land has beautiful hills and blissful rivers and valleys and three sides of it are kissed by the sea."

"All true," God admitted, "but you forgot its bloody neighbours, boyo!"

The inn shook with laughter and singing and, point made, I was welcomed into the fireside circle at last.

As I left that night the moon was out and the stars twinkled. There was no hint of the wind that had troubled me all day and I knew that if this weather held, by morning we would have radiant sunshine. So it proved and Peter told me of the second lake to try. This, again, had been a

The wind rises.

monkish stewpond and its history was reputed to go back to the Dark Ages. It was situated, he said, just beyond a fringe of woodland that would shelter it from any wind, as would the low-lying hills that surrounded it. It was primarily a trout water, he said, and for that reason alone other carp had never been stocked to augment the original wild strain. If there were wild carp in Britain, Peter vowed, they would be here in this lake.

Mammoth breakfast done with, we travelled to the water together and it was every bit as wonderful as Peter had described it. It lay, I guess about fifteen acres, in a basin of uninhabited woods and hills. The sun shone brightly above it and in the clear water I could see the richness of the bed. The odd trout flopped around the margins after emerging insects and my confidence began to soar. I was left there alone just upon nine o'clock and for seven hours little of note happened. I chose the far bank and I settled there float fishing bread flake in around five feet of water. There was no need to over-complicate matters, Peter said, for these fish had hardly ever been pursued by anglers. Three times my float dipped during the course of that day and three protesting brown trout were hustled to the net and quickly released. It was around the late afternoon sunset that I wandered up the bank towards the shallows. I had gone a hundred yards when a cloud of silt four yards from the bank caught my eye. I crouched immediately and peered down into the water. I need not tell you what I

A wonderful Welsh wildie.

5lb of Welsh muscular wildie.

saw: four carp were on their heads there, their tales just breaking the surface of the water. All looked long and mean and golden and wild! I was up there with my gear in seconds and the float had hardly settled when it tremored, cocked and was away under the surface.

Altogether, before dark totally set in, I had two wild carp from this extraordinary lake. Neither was the 15lb fish that Peter had talked about. One, I guess, was 3lb with the other perhaps scraping 5lb. Both fought manically, however, and both surely possessed every feature desirable in a wild fish. They were absolutely sleek and absolutely the shape of a river chub. Perhaps the most beautiful aspect of them was their colouration. In 99 per cent of cases I had found in the past, wild carp were a dull, smoky gun-metal colour. These fish, though, blistered gold. They were fabulous fish and when the last rays of the sun caught them, it was as though they exploded in fire. I left that lake with a feeling of deep, warm satisfaction. It was good to know that somehow I had forged this link with the past in deepest Wales. That night, talking to Peter in the hotel, I almost wondered if I need go on this quest to south-east Europe. Surely these were the original article and such a long journey would hardly be worth while. Still, I felt it necessary to both Alwyne and myself to travel and to see what I found. Who knows what adventures I would find along the way?

Another ancient Welsh wildie home.

Travel Plans

We could have flown to Alwyne Wheeler's Lake Volvi in northern Greece but we realized that if we did so we would miss a great deal of excitement on the way. For that reason, we decided to drive the couple of thousand miles across Europe and down through the Balkans. The car had to be thoroughly serviced but there was a right wheel bearing that I simply could not afford to replace. We would just have to pray that it would withstand the journey. Every scrap of tackle I possessed was loaded into the car, for although wild carp were the main reason for the journey we knew there would be interesting fish to be found all along the way. I had already corresponded a great deal with Fred Crouch about the possibilities of big European barbel and that was an intriguing subject to check out. Carp, barbel, catfish, roach, pike, zander, trout . . . whatever swam between Ostende and the Black Sea coast would be our target – especially after we had checked out the wild carp quest. We had been told that sweetcorn was difficult to obtain in Eastern Europe and raids on local supermarkets produced enough tins to have fed Norwich for a year. Tents, rods, clothes . . . I swear I could hear that weak wheel bearing groan as all the gear was stacked in.

[85]

Wild Carp in the Balkans

Undoubtedly, the whole of the Balkans teem with carp and equally surely there are massive ones to be caught. Austria, Yugoslavia, Greece, Hungry, Bulgaria, Rumania and very probably when we can get in there more freely, Albania, all hold fish of possibly up to the 90lb mark. The biggest I heard of personally upon my travels was around 88lb but equally surely these fish are generally restricted and much rarer, I feel, than even English 40lb fish.

Alwyne Wheeler is quite correct. The more remote areas of the Balkans are the cradle of wild carp. There are lakes there that are absolutely full of them. Fish average between two and five pounds – long, lean, fully scaled fish about whose ancestry there can be no doubt whatsoever. These must be absolutely original carp and their waters have no history of stocking whatsoever. There is no need for stocking as the fish are quite able to maintain their numbers in these fertile, warm waters. Breeding is prolific and that probably affects the ultimate size of these fish. I talked to many professional fisherman throughout the Balkans and from what I could gather the largest wild carp peak at about 25lb. Even so these would be amazing fish and the thought of a 25lb wildie would have made every inch of my 4,000 mile round journey worth while. The largest that I actually saw on the bank was around 11lb. Then I saw a slightly larger one break a Serbian line and a giant of some 13–15lb swim past me one morning at dawn. Had I have caught him I would have been quite sure of my genuine double-figure wildie. The largest I actually banked was just a little short of this figure but I had no complaints whatsoever. I both caught and saw some glorious wild carp, which struck me with their infinite variety of colours. The tones of these foreign fish are far richer than any I have found in Britain. Over here, wild carp tend to inhabit the farm pond-type of environment where they compete with bream or roach and as a result they are wiry, dull-coloured affairs. They seem to reflect the drab, murky nature of their environment. This is not the case in the Balkans. The waters are generally very large, rich and the fish have full opportunity to fulfil all their genetic potential in shape and colour. As to size, I am less sure.

We have to realize that fish in the Balkans – as in most countries, and not just in under-developed ones – are seen as a food resource and are killed and eaten. Balkan carp, wildies and, in the waters that hold them, big mirrors, run a constant gauntlet and it is a wise fish indeed that lives out fifteen or so years to reach its maximum size. Balkan anglers are not bad fisherman at all. In a Yugoslavian magazine I found diagrams drawn by Chris Turnbull for my own carp book. Also Andy Little's latest articles were roughly translated. Much of the tackle over there may be crude but the fisherman use several rods with multi hooks and bolt rigs and by dint of dedication achieve a good deal of success.

And, of course, methods are used beyond simple rod and line. Long lines are set by many most nights and reap rich rewards come morning. Many fisherman also use long nets which are operated by teams of boatmen. We all know that nets are not 100 per cent efficient but these men have been brought up with them and operate them with great skill.

In all probability some of the biggest wildies can be found in the more remote mountain lakes and reservoirs, which are vast, and which are situated in very sparsely populated areas. I have no doubt that fish can remain in these types of waters relatively undisturbed and attain a very large maximum size. Another possibility is to look for wild carp in some of the show-piece waters that are protected to some extent. Lake Bled is a good example of this. The town that surrounds it is quite beautiful and attracts tourists from all over Europe. Anglers are discouraged by the price of tickets and at £20 per day, few of them fish for the very large carp – admittedly of the king strain – that are known to be there.

The Balkans also hold populations of mirror carp and common carp. Faster-growing carp have been stocked into the lakes and pits around cities. The flat lands around Belgrade are a particularly good example and pits just off the River Danube are reputed to hold massive mirror carp. The tributaries of that river are dammed to provide hydroelectric power and in the extensive lake-like pieces of water that are so created I have seen one or two very big carp top in the heat of the day. These areas of water rarely see a serious angler after big fish.

However, carp fishing in the Balkans is not always easy. In one particular country I found a beautiful small lake that held some quite magnificent-looking wildies. I saw one fish cruising past that was probably 10 or 11lb and I was determined to come back the next morning at dawn. I walked past a small, white church down into a valley of woods and cornfields. Night paled, the east glowed and the sun rose and drew mists off the little pond in front of me. It was with shaking fingers that I put my gear together. The lake was only shallow and I decided as a result to try and catch the carp on the top where they had been very active the day before. I cut up a loaf and threw handfuls of crusts out on to the water. Immediately from all around the perimeter of the pool there were loud plops. To my amazement dozens of large multi-coloured frogs were

The wildie.

swimming frantically towards the crusts. I have never seen frogs like them. Some of them from tip to toe were six or seven or even eight inches long and their colours were quite startling. There were deep browns and electric blues and greens. One was bright scarlet and another was shocking yellow. It was as though I had walked into some hallucination. When a frog got to within two feet of the crusts it dived and then swam under water to within an inch of the floating bread. There it popped up and immediately pounced on the crust as if it expected it to show life and escape from it. The more pieces of bread I threw out, the more frogs appeared and to fish on the top for these wildies was quite clearly impossible.

As a result, therefore, I decided to fish on the bottom with a float and flake. I cast out under the willows on my right and immediately two frogs began to attack the float! One even managed to get a good half of it down its throat! Almost at once, however, a carp took the bait three feet beneath and the float slid away with the choking frog being pulled under the water's surface. I played the carp into my bank where it plugged deep down under my feet with the float flipping on the surface. This drove the frogs absolutely wild. They obviously believed it was some insect or animal in difficulties and eight or nine of these extraordinary amphibians immediately piled on to it while the fish was being played beneath!

A very pleasurable aspect to carp fishing in the Balkans is the way in which fishing is seen as family entertainment. Whole families appear for the day by the lakeside and the children and fathers fish while the wives read and eventually cook the catch. The scene is relaxed. Bottles of wine are drunk and from time to time everybody goes for a swim in the lake to cool off. By mid-afternoon there is a smell of cooking all along the lake shore. Way out, men are fishing in boats and they are quite obviously asleep under the high sun. In the heat people shelter under awnings and play cards and read newspapers and involve themselves in political arguments. As dusk falls the professionals arrive and begin to lay their nets. The whole scene is one of laughter and merriment and you feel that these are fisherman who really know how to live. It was on the borders of Albania that we met up with just such a professional fisherwoman and had one of the most remarkable experiences of our lives.

Life with José

We had driven many hundred of miles down the coastline and finally turned away from the Adriatic into a bleached land of gorse and scrub that levered itself up from sea-level, stone by scorched stone. What trees there were grew stunted and parched and served as a shelter for the piles of rubbish left mysteriously miles from any town. In all it was an arid wasteland, somehow sinister without the smiling effect of the sun. All day it had been cloudy and now, by the mid-afternoon, thunder rolled ceaselessly. The lake lay leaden a hundred feet below us in its basin, reached by an uncared-for track. As we ground over the pot-holes and the boulders I could hear that right wheel bearing groan and grind. The lake was vast – well over 2,000 acres and we wandered at least half a mile looking for a suitable base camp. Finally we found it. A point had been built out from the bank and deep water surrounded it. I swam out and dived to find a depth of fifteen feet just ten yards out. Everything looked good and we baited heavily with over 20lb of corn. It came on to rain torrentially which slowed every task down and it was late afternoon before the rods were positioned and camp was arranged. We were looking forward to the next few days on the water in the sure knowledge that as the corn supplies built up more and more fish would be pulled in. This seems to be the way of it on these Balkan lakes. Unless you are very lucky the fishing begins slowly, and gradually speeds up as bait is introduced. The bigger fish seemed to come in later on, pushing the smaller ones out of the way.

At this point, José arrived. A deceptively small, timid looking figure on the skyline, scantily dressed under a smeared rain coat. She rummaged on the beach to our left for a while and then looked up and said 'Go! Allez!' There was no mistaking the woman and she waved us away with wild gestures, shooing at us as though we were cattle or geese. The language barrier was inpenetrable and we asked her why repeatedly. 'Private. Go. Now.' We still hung miserably around, quite reluctant to dismantle the camp in which we had so much faith. The lake, anyway, we had been assured was free fishing. 'Police. Go. Go.' The storm crackled on and early darkness began to settle. Fifty or sixty yards from the beach was a low building, a hut of some sort, just visible in the gloom. She called and an alsatian bounded down and now at last we did move and fast. We cursed our luck that on that vast lake we should choose the one spot to be moved on from. The thought of setting up another camp in the rain and in the darkness was quite miserable. A man appeared. It was now or never. I approached him and tried to explain. 'You feesh, I tell my woman.' The pair had an argument every bit as violent as the storm over our heads but at last it was decided. 'You feesh, I tell my woman.'

The good thing about this was that José bore no malice. She accepted the verdict and set to make friends of us. At once she began to inspect our tackle and was delighted particularly with our Optonics. Bit by bit, we began to learn that José was a professional fisherwoman, living in the hut on the banks of this remote, lost lake. Her husband, it seemed, owned a shop in a far-off communist town and the profits in that were by no means enough to keep the family alive. As a result, José netted carp and put out long lines for them to supplement the income. All this we learned in just a few minutes as we were greeted as instant friends. There was no more talk of leaving or of police and in actual fact we were now accepted almost as part of the family.

There was a rope attached to a rock and this José began to pull in. She called delightedly, jumped into a rowing boat and paddled out hauling the rope in as she went. Way out in the lake I could see her lifting in two or three carp that were on the hooks of the long line. She returned with them and immediately began to de-scale the still-living fish! Soon there was even more blood on that smeared coat of hers and she threw the still-twitching, scaleless fish at our feet. These were to be our supper! We were invited up to the hut and a fire was built outside. The carp were cut into small cubes, put in a pan with plenty of herbs, salt and onion and fried there in the open air. The rain had stopped now though the atmosphere was humid and lightning continued to flicker on and off. Outside the hut was an area of rough garden where enormous tomatoes hung in profusion. These, the carp, local bread and lashings of red wine were our dinner. God knows what happened that night, but we suddenly realized it was 1 a.m. and we were all rather drunk. They would not listen to any thought of our leaving. Despite the filth, despite the stench of dead fish and rotting bait, the hut was quite homely.

In the end, we would spend several days there with José helping to lay the nets and haul in the long lines. We ate carp for breakfast, lunch and dinner and virtually all we drank was the red wine, strong enough to take the skin off our tonsils. Each night her husband came to see us, brought fresh supplies and even bought an English dictionary so that our conversation could be more varied and meaningful. I look back now on that time with José as a quite perfect one. At the time there were complications with the enormous rats that shared the hut with us, with snakes that seem to abound under every stone of the desert-like landscape around us and with the constant sight of dead or dying carp always around us. Yet, the days that passed were very warm and sun-filled, vibrant with new tastes, sensations and friendships. Never had I seen so many carp. We caught them on rod and line still, on long lines and in nets and in those few days I must have handled several hundred fish – all wildies, none over 10lb, but all brilliantly coloured and exciting just to gaze upon. This massive lake that straddled the borders of two countries must have been the type of water that Alwyne Wheeler had in mind as the cradle of wild carp. I felt here that our quest was truly fulfilled and that if there is such a thing as an original carp it was here.

As the days wore on José introduced us to her friends, mostly professional fisherman, all of whom seemed to live a wild and free type of life. They all embraced us as immediate friends and shared instinctively their boats, their knowledge, their wine and their stories. From them, we learnt that the lake held far more than carp. Often the talk turned to '*som*' and at last, intrigued, I figured out that these were in fact catfish. The common way of catching them was to go out by boat at night into the shallows. A large, dead carp would be put on a stake which was lashed to a leather thong. The angler held the thong and worked the dead carp vigorously up and down near the bottom. The catfish would be attracted by the commotion, grab the carp and find the stake lodged in its throat. The angler could then pull the snared catfish into the boat. In theory this obviously worked well most times, but in practice, occasionally, things could go wildly wrong. Only a few weeks before we arrived a carp was taken and the angler was pulled overboard by the disappearing catfish. The thong had been tied to his wrist and he could not escape in time. Two days later the body of the catfish was found, the fish choked to death on the carp. A leather thong's length away from him was the drowned angler.

The other way these people fished for catfish was with a long line and a carp for a bait. I was madly keen to see a Balkan catfish and I pestered José for her to try. She was not at all keen. Carp were easier to catch, more saleable and could be eaten. *Som* were big, not very plentiful and could be dangerous. However, we were friends and she would deny us nothing. The third night of our stay a 4lb carp was kept alive as bait for the night catfishing session! A monstrous hook was put through the back of the bait and ten feet up the line a rock about the size of a brick was attached as a weight to keep the carp in mid-water. The line was a rope and we rowed out over 100 yards before pitching the bait and the weight overboard in water that José said was twenty or twenty-five feet deep. Back on shore the rope was coiled up and the end tied round a massive rock. We all sat on the beach that night and ate our carp supper and drank under the eastern stars. The rope twitched constantly all night long as the carp worked way off in the darkening lake. Never, though, was it taken and in the morning we rowed out and collected it as lively as we had let it down the night before. Waste not, want not! José killed it and we ate the poor beast for breakfast.

The following night followed along the same lines only this time, if anything, the bait was even larger! Sadly, dawn again signalled another fruitless night. José took some persuading to fish the third night but at last she agreed. Now the bait was truly enormous. She sorted out a carp that could not have weighed less that 8 or 9lb and this giant was taken out into the deep water. I felt sure the bait was too big and the coiled rope was continually being pulled as the fish managed to shift even the large rock tethering it to the bottom. At 3 a.m. something dramatic happened. The rope on the beach simply hissed out into the water. Within seconds it was tight to the boulder and twanging like a bow strong. With whoops of excitement we all bundled into a couple of boats, my privilege being to row José in the fighting boat. I will never quite forget that battle! José sat hunched in the front of the boat, holding the rope grimly and hauling it in yard by yard whenever ground was given. At first I rowed madly and then once, pausing for breath, I realized that in fact the boat was moving

The first focus of attention for a Victorian lad, perhaps. A lovely example of a hand-painted quill float 'the link which connects the contemplative man with wonders of the deep'. H.T. Sheringham. An Open Creel. Wild carp fishing should be done on the float.

by itself, towed by an unseen force below. My own paltry efforts were nothing compared with the strength of this monster. Sometimes the fish took us out into the middle and then it would sulk until José pulled it and aggravated it into some sort of action again. Up and down the lake we went in this way for two hours until dawn was beginning to show. All the while José was quiet and her husband in the next boat simply followed us watching intently. At last there was a cry of excitement and I looked around to see the rock-weight breaking the surface. Whatever we had on our line was now only ten feet beneath the boat. Sometimes that rock disappeared back under the wave but minute by minute it was coming further from the water until it was actually in the boat itself.

Then, my God, I saw it! Two feet beneath the surface swam a thing! In the half light I had trouble focusing on such an immense creature. I would think that for at least a minute I was incapable of gauging the size of fish that I was so close to. One by one, however, the statistics began to click in my brain. Our boat was ten feet long and this monster was longer than that. The head, which I could now see clearly was well over two feet wide! At one point one of the feelers was over the side of the boat and moving, twitching over the boards and in among the ropes. All this will remain with me for the rest of my life and yet I only saw that fish for two minutes at the most. It swam along with us quietly for this short while and then thrashed and tried to dive again for the bottom. José screamed to her husband, there was a hurried discussion, he pulled a knife, and with one stroke cut the straining rope. Everything was over, and we were all silent.

[93]

I remained speechless an hour or more. At first I could not understand why we did not continue the battle and tire the fish to the point of exhaustion. Little by little the husband explained the fish was too large to boat safely and too large to be of saleable value. It was simply a point of interest that they had caught it for us, to show us that the lake did hold monsters. I will always regret bitterly that we did not land and photograph that fish but at least I saw it and at least I was involved in one of the most exciting battles imaginable.

Of course, it is in my mind to go back again. I know now what that lake holds and I feel it is just possible to catch creatures like this on rod and line. Shark tackle, a large enough boat and immense patience should make it possible to play such a fish to a standstill. Perhaps this would not be fair as it must be debatable whether a fish would recover from such a strain in such warm waters, but one day, I feel the concept must be tried out. How big was that catfish? Obviously I have not got a clue myself. All I can say is that I have never seen a living creature like it and I realize just how far I had come from that boy who once regarded a 4oz roach as a monster!

Visions of Europe

Just about the only graffiti we saw throughout Europe was written in English. Perhaps we were unlucky, perhaps we took the wrong routes but even 2,000 road miles from Dover, the insults and the swear words were always in English. A bridge in high, interior Austria was plastered with obscenities about Arsenal and foreigners. A café wall in northern Yugoslavia was splattered with comments that would disgust anybody. Why?

The political barriers had just come down in Eastern Europe and the autoroutes all over the west were now flooded with cars from East Germany (as it was), Poland and Hungary. These were tiny, old, slow and belched out exhaust fumes as they trundled along in the wake of the BMWs and Mercedes. They were invariably crammed with passengers looking, one felt, with awe at a richness and opulence they had never seen before. How did they feel, these aged East Germans, looking now on this land of wealth and riches? Did they feel cheated out of a life of material possessions by war, by politics and by the inflexibility of those that had governed them? At their age, many of them retired, the thaw between East and West had come too late for them ever to own, for example, a majestic Audi.

[94]

I met one very fat fisherman on the banks of a lake in central Europe. We had no common language whatsoever – only the man's tackle. Virtually everything he possessed had been made by Drennan and he was massively proud. Every article he held up for me to observe and admire – as if I did not have them myself or had not used them for years past. Every minute he would grin and say proudly in a loud guttural accent, 'Drennan'. Drennan was some type of god out there and many times I was asked for his address so that anglers could write to him direct and obtain his tackle far more cheaply than was possible after all the huge import duties put on it. I had taken my own Drennan rods with me and these were worshipped by anglers from Germany southwards. When the fat man could not buy Drennan he improvised and many of his own floats were home-made. One range in particular consisted of floats of over two feet long and capable of carrying 6 or 7oz of weight! He demonstrated how far these could be cast and how well he could control them. My mind went back to the Trent. Otter used similar-sized weapons on the tidal Trent for the big barbel there in the nineteenth century. Certainly my fat friend could cast over a hundred yards, control the float and it would still be visible, riding proudly above the waves. This was the float that he used to get out colossal distances for big bream shoals and he showed me a tattered and faded photograph of a 14-pounder landed this way.

Yugoslavia is a troubled place and its different republics quarrel interminably among themselves. Taxes are high and the standard of living outside the tourist centres is poor. As a result, many of those with the intelligence or the initiative leave to work abroad. I met one such man who had spent all his working life in Canada and now had returned to the homeland to retire. He was venerated in the village as a man who had travelled, could speak English and had vast wealth. It took us two days to obtain an interview with him and he treated us to Canadian Club Whisky, his boat on the lake, and dinner at one of the premier restaurants. He was proud to show off his English and to talk about his life in the Canadian outback. Once we had been seen out in the town with this man we too were treated as minor celebrities. The news got round that we knew Jak and from then on preferential treatment was always ours.

As we moved further east we began to see more and more of the cities that had been shaped by communism. They were drab, dirty and the plaster was off the buildings. Tenement blocks predominated and washing hung from the balconies. The streets were littered with cars that would have been scrapped in the West years before. Paper blew everywhere and litter was left uncollected for weeks on end. The cafés were mean affairs with few or no luxuries for sale. Hygiene was poor and any public toilet was to be avoided. Many of the rivers were polluted and ran between concreted, canalized banks, often dirty blue or orange in colour. Around the towns hung a constant smell of chemicals and grime. Every civic building was made ugly and functional. Everything was second-rate – the department stores, the buses, the trains and the petrol stations which, of course, sell no unleaded petrol. It was this obvious lack of care for the environment that was so shocking. I spoke to one pleasant Hungarian trout fisherman who was doing his best to secure some supper from a river that ran through a two-mile rubbish tip. This was hardly the Test of Halford and Skues! In these little-seen areas of Eastern Europe it is as though the last fifty years have been wasted and possibly now the landscape has been irretrievably scarred by the shoddy building of the post-war years.

In central Europe, however, I came across the most wonderful trout rivers and was pleased to have had my fly tackle with me. The waters of Austria and southern Germany were wickedly clear and quick and catching the big trout and grayling from them was a nightmare. I saw one grayling that could not have weighed less than 4 or 5 lb, and every morning he would be at the same position – the lower bridge. I would try for the whole day long with every trick that I knew and I never even came close to interesting him. Everybody wanted him and everybody tried for him but nobody had yet succeeded in even hooking him. The trout I found somewhat easier and at dawn one morning I hooked and lost a veritable monster that took me twenty yards down river, into weed, through some trailing branches and down a weir, breaking me comprehensively in the process. That fish was 8lb at least.

Carinthian River

On the return from the Balkans we felt in need of some civilization again. In the very south of Austria runs one of the major tributaries that eventually joins the Danube. This huge river flows through gorges and across a flood plain that is gloriously decorated with churches, shrines, whitewashed houses and spires that glint in the almost continual sunshine. After much of what we had seen in the communist East this was a veritable Garden of Eden. The beautiful mountain ranges and castles, cafés, terraces, flowers, orchards and butterflies all made it the most colourful and welcoming of havens. There was even an old toy maker who spent most of the day outside his shop of faded wooden dolls and rocking horses. But of course it was the river that interested me the most.

Even this, just a tributary of Europe's great river, was massive. Every few miles it was dammed by hydroelectric works and so the overall effect was to produce a few miles of rapid water beneath each station that gradually slowed to become massively calm and lake-like above the next one. There was, therefore, every variety of water imaginable and the stocks of fish that the river held were immense. In awe, I was assured that these were the potential weights of the fish species found in this river: catfish to 300lb, barbel to 17lb, pike to 50lb, zander to 20lb, chub to 9lb, roach to 4lb, trout to 25lb, and bream to 22lb! How much of this could I believe? Where should I begin? What should I set out to hunt?

It was a strange fish that caught my attention first. Wandering the faster water and peering into the milky green depths on that first morning, I was immediately attracted by shoals of medium-sized fish that were feeding very close in on large rocks. At first they looked rather like a cross between dace and roach and they were twisting vigorously as though sucking minute insects or weed off the boulders. I enquired of the local anglers and realized that these were nase. A nase is also called a snout fish because of its big top upper lip – almost mullet-like – which serves to scrape weed off the bottom. I immediately tried for them with the over-heavy gear that I had with me and although I drifted bait after bait through shoals of fish that I could clearly see, I never caught a thing. I realized that a radical rethink was necessary. I returned to the car and came back with gear that would be more suitable for trotting for dace on the Wensum in the winter. A small stick float, a 2lb line, a size 16 hook and half a grain of corn now tripped its way through the nase shoals. Action was immediate. The float had only travelled five yards before it jabbed down to the first fish. I have heard it said that nase do not fight. Where that rumour came from I cannot guess, because these fish went absolutely wild. In all, I had half a dozen using the new technique, to a maximum of about 3lb in weight. All were quite wonderful-looking fish and had obviously never been caught before.

The rest of that day was simply spent exploring the vast river. I found a tremendous lagoon in the middle reaches where the water had slowed down considerably and widened out to flood an old forest. In there I saw some splendid chub up to 4 or 5lb and a pike that approached 20lb stalking some rudd. Even lower down where the river widened out to something like 200 yards in width I saw a shoal of enormous bream priming on the surface mid-way out. From what I could see, not a fish was below double figures. Beneath a bridge I saw a shoal of roach dimpling the surface with zander hitting into them. Just above one of the dams I found almost a mini-lake created and in there I was told very large catfish lurked to be caught at night. Beneath this dam the water roared out in fury and it was there that, apparently, some of the biggest barbel were to be found. All in all I hardly knew where to start that next day. Truly this was a bewildering river full of character and full of enormous fish.

Let me say that I was almost defeated by the variety of what I saw. Only having a few days I virtually panicked and did not perhaps make the rational decisions that I should have done. What I did do, however, did turn out to be satisfactory. My decision was to stick to the fast water below the hydroelectric works and to swim-feeder corn there for whatever should come along. The decision was, to an extent, successful though I regret now not putting more time in for the pike and catfish of the slower reaches. I suppose the best thing that I can do is simply tell the story of the day that I enjoyed best.

It poured from early morning; only the second rain we had seen in many weeks away. From the very first cast there was action. A big feeder, a Drennan rod, 5lb line, a size 12 hook and three grains of corn were all the tools that I needed all day long. The rod tip simply went round and round again. God knows how many pounds of fish I had during the course of that day but I went through well over two dozen cans of corn. On top of that six loaves of bread were used to plug the open feeder. I was working constantly, for it was unusual to wait even a minute for a bite. All the fish that I caught were in perfect condition and all fought very well in the enormous push of water. At this point, I was fishing in twenty feet, thirty yards from the bank, with a flow of often three to four miles per hour. It was exciting fishing indeed!

So what did I catch that amazing day? In short I took silver bream of over 4lb and a common bream of 8lb. I had barbel to 5lb and saw one roll that was around about 8 lb. I had many nase that seemed confident enough to take the big bait on heavy tackle as a swim built up. One of them was just over 4lb. I had several trout to 3lb and a grayling that touched 2½lb. I had a pike of 10lb that attacked a small roach on the way in. In mid-morning I located a shoal of roach. The first one weighed 2lb 2oz and the second was 2lb 10oz. These were quite magnificent fish and there was no doubt whatsoever about their identity – true roach to the last scale count. The 2lb 10oz fish went back and the next cast produced something even more spectacular. From its fight I knew it could not be a roach but it seemed as though it was! In my net and on my scales lay a 4lb

4lb 3oz of fish, too slim to be a roach perhaps . . .

3oz fish! At the time, I looked at this fish carefully as you can imagine and decided on the river bank that it was a true roach. I was worried about the slimness of body but that had been a characteristic of the fish caught previously and I considered it probably the natural shape in such fast water. However, I took what photographs I could in the driving rain and poor light, and returned the huge fish.

That roach – if roach it was – should have been the highlight of the day, but very late on, as I was about to pack up – sodden like blotting paper – far out an enormous silver fish rose high from the water. Three times it jumped, a bar of silver which I guessed to be four feet long. During the day I had made a friend and I asked him what the fish could be. There was no doubt in his voice: 'huchen!' I had even seen one of the huge land-locked salmon of central Europe!

The potential of rivers like these is enormous and during these few days I merely scratched the surface. Like Fred Crouch, I am still dubious about true potential barbel size. It does worry me that the European anglers continue to kill and eat everything they catch but it does seem that on waters as vast as these, many fish can escape and live on to a staggering maturity. The river is amazingly prolific and there can be no doubt that predatory fish do extraordinarily well there. I have no doubt whatsoever about the potential size of pike from this type of river. On one of my explorations I talked to an elderly couple who were about to embark on a boat fishing trip. They showed me the picture of a pike the gentleman had caught the previous week. They said it weighed 40lb and I would not disbelieve them from the photograph that I saw. I saw more photographs of zander up to 16lb and, believe me again, these weights must have been accurate.

I know I must travel to my Carinthian river again. It is a place I love and was a place where I was welcomed by everyone I met. Most of all, though, I know that I have hardly begun to explore the potential of this river. As far as the barbel go, on future trips I will experiment well away from the areas that are reputedly 'hot'. My feeling is that the barbel are well thinned out by local anglers, who take everything for their pot at home. I do feel it possible, however, that in the less fished, more remote areas very large barbel could exist.

I will also continue to look at the roach potential. When I returned to England, I had the photographs processed and the slimness of the fish continued to worry me. I sent a photograph to Alwyne Wheeler along with a report of my Balkan carp adventures, and he agreed that the fish could have been a roach chub hybrid – as I had surmised. My gut feeling remains that the fish was a true roach, however, and certainly the smaller ones which I landed before that giant definitely were. Even a 2lb 10oz roach is a super fish and certainly points strongly towards massive fish being present.

As it is the predators that interest me the most, I would undoubtedly take a boat with an electric engine and Humminbird recorder. I would catch lives baits and troll these just off the bottom or in mid-water. There are many miles of water to try which have hardly seen a bait before and I am quite convinced pike and zander of massive proportions live there. I would stay at one of the little colourful pensions, eat the most fabulous food in the cafés in the evening, drink the fine south Austrian wine and meet up again with those anglers who helped me so much and become so dear to me in so short a space of time. It is hard to think of a more glorious place to fish.

4

Indian Adventure

The Story of a Fishing Film

Over the years, angling and television have not generally mixed well and there have been some disasters that have made every true angler squirm in his or her seat. However, there were exceptions, such as the *Out of Town* series of programmes made by Jack Hargreaves and also those dramatizations of the Arthur Ransome *Rod and Line* stories starring Michael Hordern. These notable attempts were followed in 1987 by the first programmes in the *Go Fishing* series made for Anglia TV by Norwich tackle dealer John Wilson. John was an instant success. His warm personality, rich sense of humour, use of words, and enthusiasm for fish and fishing skill combined to produce excellent television. It was not only anglers who became involved; for the first time a fishing programme became family viewing. Anglia sold nation-wide. Audience ratings soared and John became something of a star, stopped in the street and even, he once told me, lusted after by women!

The success of *Go Fishing* interested other television companies and in 1988 the independent film makers, Best Endeavours, managed to interest Granada in an idea for an extensive angling adventure set in the Himalayas. In this pursuit of the legendary mighty mahseer I was to be presenter and fisherman. In the television world, however, interest and contracts are quite different matters. Impossibly large sums of money are involved in taking a camera crew to an alien continent for months and Granada wanted to be quite sure of the product they were investing in.

For this reason in July 1988 a pilot film was arranged in north-west Scotland. For a week, Peter, the director, and I made our reconnaissance and then the producers, a crew of three and Roger Miller appeared for five days of filming. The target was naturally ferox and equally naturally I failed to catch one of those. Fortunately a char or two, a smaller trout and a grilse provided sufficient action to interest Granada further. Personally, my own performances improved from the woeful to the just acceptable and looked almost likely to hook an American joint sponser for the Asian expedition. In that eventful week, I had learned film jargon, how to act reasonably naturally in front of a camera and how crews can drink until 4 a.m. each and every night and still produce excellent work the following day. In short, Miller and I both rather enjoyed being 'stars' and I looked forward to a further and larger-scale attempt.

The autumn of 1988 proved to be a frenzied time of discussion and negotiation, hopes and disappointments, meetings and general hustle and bustle all around the country. Indecision lasted over the New Year and into the spring. Only in May, at long last, did a contract actually land for August. We had eight weeks to prepare passports, visas, injections, clothing and tackle. The injections were the worst and my arm grew sorer and sorer until on one fateful afternoon in a London traffic jam one of them reacted badly upon me. An ambulance appeared out of nowhere and I was whisked off to the casualty ward of a hospital to recover slowly over the next few hours. India, it seemed, had already begun its assault!

I had not been to India before and obviously the hopes and fears of a giant TV company could not ride on a whim of mine alone. Into the fray, therefore, was drawn Paul Boote, then the owner of Graham Phillips rods

Our Indian assistants.

and a veteran of nearly a dozen Indian trout and mahseer trips. Negotiations with Paul were hardly easier than those that had taken place with Granada. Paul is a very intelligent, independent man who realizes the value of his knowledge and was determined not to sell it cheaply. Correctly, we were made co-presenters with exactly equal standing within the film. Had it not been for Best Endeavours, Granada would have not put up the money. But for Paul, it is doubtful if we would have found anything to catch or to film.

So it was that on 11 August 1989 at 3 p.m. I was on board a British Airways flight bound for New Delhi and a new challenge in my angling life.

Good Companions

Linda: Producer. Tall and rather gaunt. A middle-aged lady with immense experience in the film and finance business. Constantly cool and calm in a land of heat and pressure, she made all arrangements for this long shoot impeccably. Any problems arose only out of general Indian

Peter, the Himalayas and Ganges beneath.

apathy, bureaucratic incompetence or the tensions in a country ruled by religious, racial, political and economic problems. In short – kind, caring, and generous. She even forgave me my foolishness when I threw away a return ticket on an internal Indian flight!

Peter: Director. Late twenties. First major chance with an important film. Determined to succeed and worked with driving intensity whilst at the same time keeping composure and humour. Constantly inventive, appreciative and supportive. Always had the affection of a very professional crew and gradually, too, won their respect. Boundless energy. Jogged with me at 8,000 feet in Kashmir. Played football with native children everywhere. Climbed. Fished. Swam. Relished Indian food until his eyes popped.

Frenyi: Peter's Assistant. Inexperienced in films but provided vital liaison with the crowds that gathered wherever cameras were pitched. Without her herding of the thousands, the crew would have been overrun in minutes. Constant source of calm and interpreter of a thousand alien customs.

John: 'The Cam'. A cameraman of immense experience and talent. Very

John 'the Cam' makes the most of his lens.

skilled technically with a great feel for shots. A child of the 60s. Lover of long hair and late-night laughter. Genuine warmth. Crazy humour and the man to defuse tension and smooth any discord. Adored by native children and followed by tribes of them as he paddled across the Ganges sands swathed in a red skirt to protect his burning legs.

Joe: Assistant Cameraman. Mid-twenties and vastly experienced world-wide. Much in demand for painstaking efficiency and natural flair. Very much the style of a Londoner. Only lost this when he slipped and fell into a pile of human excrement! Nice ability to appraise people in challenging situations with quiet humour of his own.

George: Sound Man. Thirties. Short. Puckish. Eyes screwed up tight till midday. Slept in a nightshirt, otherwise a complete professional! Sense of fun only disappeared around fools or incompetents – often me. Periods of gluttonous appetite. Four helpings at dinner were usual for George. A home-loving man who constantly and reluctantly travels the world to keep his much-missed family.

Paul: Presenter and Angler. Late thirties. Articulate. Intense about everything he might do. Complex man with probing, alert mind. A charismatic and demanding companion. Vastly experienced traveller and angler with a deep interest in world culture, music and literature.

Dinesh: Born in Nepal. Our guide and on-the-ground organizer. Early thirties. Lovable man. Small, strong, wiry with encyclopedic knowledge of the high lands. A trained biologist and expert in Himalayan cultures. Occasional explosions of temper add weight to his generally calm administration. A cook. An angler. A guitarist, photographer and a highly accomplished man.

The Mahseer: Our target. Half carp, half barbel, it can grow to over five feet. A famed fighter, 'beside whom the tarpon is a herring' (Rudyard Kipling). A traveller of the rivers and the king of the River Ganges.

Kashmir

We had to arrive early in India for we could not risk the monsoon being over, the rivers having fallen and all the mahseer having migrated back

A pre-independence monster mahseer.

The less opulent houseboats on the river Ghelum.

into the impenetrable Ganges. We arrived, however, too early and
northern India was still awash. The Ganges and its tributaries were at full
bore. For this reason we entered Kashmir where the rains are lighter and
where we knew we would have sport with trout and possibly carp.

If a carp angler fancied the honeymoon of his or her dreams then I
would suggest a week on a houseboat in Srinigar, the ancient capital of
Kashmir. These houseboats, the better ones anyway, are fit for any bride
or groom. They float like castles, exquisitely carved, decorated and
furnished with lavish bedrooms and living-rooms. Each one has its
houseboy who cleans and serves you tea on the veranda where the water
washes at the steps. He will cook you dinner too or order a taxi to take
you into the bustling old city where there are hotels and restaurants
overlooking the river, the fabulous parks and gardens. It is well worth
waking at dawn and travelling by water taxi across the lakes where the
floating vegetable market is held. Traders from all across the vale of
Kashmir gather in their boats to sell the food for the stirring city. Crafts
full of flowers and shining vegetables pole past you on the way as they
hurry to the meeting point where rupees pile like mountains on the grey-
green lagoon. The houseboy will have breakfast ready for you on your
return, served either under the chandelier of the dining-room or on the

On the way to the vegetable market.

The locals fish for carp.

roof of the boat where you can watch the sun climb over the kingfishers and the awakening lake.

Already the carp angler in you will have seen possibilities. There are small fish in the weeds everywhere but at night you will have heard the slurps and slobberings in the lilies beside the boat and perhaps see a back come out in the moonlight. On the way to the vegetable market you will have seen huge bow-waves here and there and the reeds in the narrow channels bent back by big dark shapes. The vast run of the carp is small but big fish and huge ones do exist in the quieter areas where they take sanctuary awaiting the night. You stalk by punt, casting a piece of bread into a hole in the weeds twenty yards away from you. Pole gently through the quiet bays or out into the middle of the lake well away from bankside disturbance and there you will find fish. And all the time, your beloved can bathe in sunshine or buy fabulous silks from the water salesman.

Should you tire of this, like us, pick up a fly rod and travel over the plains to the trout streams of the mountains. You live in a camp and fish for trout at 8,500 feet perhaps in a snow melt river that runs like a turquoise train. You wade in it and the temperatures are little above

Midnight, a full moon and carp loop around the houseboats.

Great carp live in the bays.

Carping Kashmir style.

Kashmir trouting is all mountain goat work.

freezing. It is athletic fishing and you make small casts across and down and twitch a heavily weighted fly back across pools the size of a dining table. There is an infinite variety of water, all gushing and sparkling under blue skies and dazzling sunshine. The trout are frequently small, sometimes to 2lb but here and there glint the sides of big fish indeed. Takes are savage in the white water often just beneath the rod tip and many of the fish spend more time in the air than in their own element. Wading is an essential part of the game if you are going to get to the best, rarely fished pieces of water. After a morning you feel tired, numbed and cut but every second has been worth while and you can guarantee fish to cook over an open fire that evening. You are accompanied constantly by the Kashmiri people. There will be women carrying firewood on their heads and shoulders or small boys following you at a respectful distance. Men will lean over every bridge yelling and whistling and offering advice in their own barely understood tongue.

Everywhere you will go with a gillie. These are wrinkled tanned men of the river and they know their beats pebble by pebble. Their only words of English are 'feesh' or 'leetle feesh' or 'beeg feesh'. Sometimes you get a sentence from them: 'No sah – no put eem back, sah' or 'Kill eem and eat!' None will let you carry an item of gear and all spring from rock to rock like wizened goats. They will run after a hooked fish for you as though their life depends on the tip of 20 rupees or 80 pence. All smile a toothless grin at the sight of a hooked fish and all bemoan the lost big one as a tragedy. Nothing is too much bother for them. They will climb trees or wade rapids to detach a fly. They inspect your tackle with reverence and point to a fly that you would normally never try but which takes a trout at the very first cast. They accompany you happily from dawn to dusk, snatching odd naps at pools, lying fast asleep under trees until you stir them into waking. They keep away the children and youths that gather at the village bridges or washing points and who cheer and clap when a sparkling Kashmir trout is hoisted ashore. All this is a sporting pantomime that absorbs you utterly into Indian life and makes you a hundred friends within minutes.

Above all, these gillies are useful. At first you resent the intrusion and you want to fish privately. But then you accept them as a part of Indian life. They show you the tiny pools that you would overlook and even point to the stones that you need to stand upon. They take you miles through terrain you would lose yourself in and all for a daily wage of 35 rupees – much less than a gallon of petrol in Britain. All this poverty is around you yet you know you can trust £500 worth of fishing and camera equipment to them safe in the knowledge they would die rather than lose it.

You soon realize that trout fishing is important here. Kashmir has huge numbers of people relying on limited resources. It might be difficult to accept the gillies carrying your tackle and sorting out your tangles but you must realize that they need the job. This is a land where jobs must be made, however tiny, however menial, or people starve. It's good that the trout fishing is organized, for each beat has it gillies and this generates life for the entire village. These men are paid £1.40 a day and perhaps pick up enough tips to take this to £2. This means that they are highly paid and respected in an area where the average wage can be around £100 a year.

Camp life is ecstasy. The tents are comfortable and the food is prepared fresh over the fire. No one seems to fall ill and the temperatures are perfect for the European. It is in the cities of India and Kashmir that illness abounds. Let us presume you are recently married; illness will test that marriage early. When I awoke one fateful morning at 4 a.m. I knew what it was to be ill. In thirty-six hours I lost over a stone in weight and seemed at times glued to a toilet that was far from clean. I was sick in the street and I lay like a corpse in the sun. Tending to a partner like this would soon show how strongly love shines.

Paul Boote looks pensive.

We stayed in Kashmir for over a week, telephoning each day to the Ganges region for weather reports. At last it appeared that the rains showed signs of petering away and rather sadly we left that high, fresh mountain camp, bound for Delhi once more. From Delhi we would travel by bus to the heart of our mission.

Visions of India

Indian signs are not always totally without mistake and charm. For example, a postcard of the famous fort in Srinigar proclaims that 'Hari Parbat Fart in background'. I was amused by the houseboat on the river Ghelum that offered 'Private rooms. Toilets – flesh systems'. 'The Water Treatment Plant Bumzoo' also conjured up certain images . . .

We offered a chair to a Himalayan sadhu or holy man. He had not sat down for twenty-five years, he said, and he saw no need to start for us.

Three policemen appeared on a Ganges beach. They told us that a few villages down river a leopard had leapt through the door of a house and gone roaring into the kitchen. The terrified villagers locked the door and left it barred in there, growling, for thirty-six hours. Then they assembled

A view of Himalayan rivers.

all their neighbours with sticks and stones, unlocked the door and the big cat ran the gauntlet back into the forest. The family dog had been asleep in the kitchen. All that was left of it was an ear.

I met a colonel in the Nepali armed forces. He stated quite firmly that today armies are only present to cope with the insanity and aggression of the world's civilian populations. He also told me that eating a banana a day would prevent me from getting sick. It seems banana feeds the bugs in the stomach and stops them getting the vital organs.

Probably the most picturesque of all the beautiful villages in Kashmir possessed a path that led to the river. It skirted a gorge where a platform was fastened with a large hole in its middle. Beneath it was a pile of human dung ten feet high. The village women queued to use it at 5 a.m. and the men a couple of hours later when their breakfasts would be nearly prepared. The fishing bungalow we stayed at had a toilet built into a small shed out over a stream. From there the stream ran ten yards into a school playground.

Once I was awoken at 3.30 a.m. by a shuffling at the door of my tent. The moon was just bright enough to silhouette two bending figures. Peter had also been alarmed. A shout from the next tent and the pair made off, tripping over the guy ropes. 'Thieves', the camp staff said scornfully next morning. The pair had stolen my soap . . .

Through a great deal of India, you will be regularly surrounded by people begging and it is rather up to you if you respond or not. 'No' said very firmly with the wave of the hand is generally understood and the poor soul often wanders off. Yet, there is the other view, namely that a supply of two rupee notes can, in fact, do a great deal of good for a number of people. Two rupees represents about eight pence in English money and a good meal to a mother with her wild-eyed infant. Perhaps we should consider that. At the same time, you will have to learn to haggle over every tiny matter. Few prices are fixed and the Indian expects to bargain for his services or wares. If you do not want the goods almost continually put before you, tell their owners firmly. If you do, beat the price down to a level where you will not be laughed at. You do not haggle, however, in book shops. In India, learning is sacred.

Old Mr Goffhara has, or at least had, the finest tackle den in Kashmir. The building stands off the Bund, the riverside promenade that runs through Srinigar and is large, dark and imposing. The family have owned the shop for generations and sixty years ago won the coveted Hardy's agency. Those were the great times. In the 1920s and 1930s hugh brown trout and mahseer were to be had in Kashmir and the shop boomed. The war, independence and the partition of India marked the shop's downfall. The white sportsman left and the Indians exploited the rivers by illegal means. Tackle was little called-for then or, sadly, even now. Also massive import duties prevent him stocking the shop in any meaningful way. Now Mr Goffhara sits on a dusty, antiquated pile of green heart rods and old creaking centre pins with huge hooks and spoons that date from the long-gone Kashmir mahseer days. Terrorism in Kashmir has led to a fall in tourism and on the very day we met, a bomb had been placed at a street fruit store. Thirty were injured and one was dead. Mr Goffhara's son is a doctor in the West and when the old man dies or retires – and he is well into an Indian summer – I fear Srinigar will have lost a true sporting memory of the Raj and the great days of Himalayan sport fishing.

Around midnight a boat appeared out of the darkness of Nagin Lake and an English voice called 'hello' and 'help'. The man tied his craft to our houseboat and sprawled on the veranda. He was in his early twenties and dressed in the clothes of a 1960s hippy. He was totally 'done in' and asked for a coffee. It appeared he was utterly out of money and needed to get home for the start of the university term. He offered to sell us drugs and we refused; he was playing a dangerous game. However, we wanted to help so we gave him what cash we had in our pockets. We also offered him a bed for the night but instead he went off, God knows where, into the darkness we never saw him again.

Learning about Mahseer

The coach groaned across the plains of northern India. They were vast, and they were filthy. They crawled horizontally from one shimmering horizon to another. For hundreds of miles I knew that a pane of glass and a fluke of birth kept me from one of the most hopeless and depressed places on earth. Sunset came and did nothing to redeem that journey. Now the plains simply glowed like a pulsating and a burning hell.

Our destination was the foothills of the Himalayas and when they appeared they came like saviours from the flat plains behind us. There it was, in the sheeting rain, the old hill station of Dehra Dun, the home of the legendary mahseer men of history. Before independence, the town had been a military and administrative centre and the mahseer rivers had run close by for those Raj rulers to enjoy. But all that was a long time ago. The mahseer and sahibs have all disappeared and the Raj itself is nothing but a white elephant of colonial buildings, dissolving slowly in the monsoon.

A monsoon is not a rain at all but a hail of tiger teeth that is dangerous to endure. Between the first and third of September it closed in on our hotel and it raised the level of the Ganges by feet. It destroyed villages and it cost lives. It seemed to us then that it wiped out any chance of the film's success. It was curious sitting for hours on end in a hotel like that. There was nothing outside but the rain and nothing whatsoever to walk to see. The hotel bar was dowdy and once we saw a rat clamber laboriously to the ceiling. We had no real desire to drink again, endlessly, with men we had been with for three whole weeks. In some ways, it was like a scene from a Graham Greene or Evelyn Waugh novel – all peeled paint and morose talk of home, complaints of bad food, slow waiters and the failure of, at best, a semi-existent phone network.

Before I left for India I knew that there would be times like this when all that I would be able to do would be to keep my head down and not think about time; simply to get on with the job. Long before this I had cast off my watch and by the time we reached Dehra Dun I was only thinking in terms of light and dark, days and weeks and no longer in that painful dimension of hours and minutes. It is hard now to describe the drabness that surrounded that time. But then, the second afternoon, though the clouds were ever deeper down, a ray of light suddenly appeared. We had arranged an interview with Lieutenant-Colonel Morris Metha. We travelled to his bungalow, paddled through the rain and there found the original mahseer hero.

Metha is in his late seventies and is perhaps the epitome of the north Indian mahseer man. In a long life on the River Ganges and the tributaries he has had scores of fish to over 70lb. Metha had seen these rivers before their decline and known what the once-great sport of mahseer fishing was like. Even today he makes his own tackle, and a line of green plugs hung in the kitchen. He explained, with a twinkle in his eye, that the scale effect on them was paint sprayed through a mosquito net. He showed us how he made his own spinners with the use of an antique metal press. Still, nearly eighty, he is a man who is desperate for British tackle in this now starved outpost. Paul, to his credit, said that he would leave a rod and reel when or even if, we were ever to leave. Obviously I knew that mahseer had existed in the past. I had seen photographs and I had read books and I had talked to Paul. But all this was in the security of England and now to be in this bungalow, under the pelting monsoon with this frail old angler, brought home to me the enormity of what we were trying to do. At one stage, Mrs Metha took me out into the garden where we saw cobras slithering under the big wet leaves and I knew that here I had everything to learn. I went back into the lounge where Paul and Metha were sitting and I listened and I learned about the mahseer. Everything that I now tell came from that conversation and I related it as best I can.

The mahseer is now a rare creature and the damming of rivers has destroyed the runs of spawning fish. Heavy netting pressure and the use of dynamite have destroyed scores of miles. India has become industrialized and pollution has crucified mahseer rivers. The deforestation of mountains has lead to soil erosion and rapid run–off which has destabilized the spawning beds even further. Many historic mahseer spawning sites are now places of memory only.

Metha sat almost bird–like on his settee and looked at us like an emaciated sparrow. His voice was one of warning and yet one of warmth and optimism. Locating mahseer now is difficult but possible. He knew the dangers and difficulties that faced us and yet he was confident that they could be overcome. He knew that the monsoon is unpredictable in the north and this very fact of weather could be our undoing. Remember that the mahseer run up the Ganges, and leave it to ascend the tributaries during the monsoon when the waters are high. They remain on their spawning beds throughout the rains and then, as the clouds clear and the waters begin to drop and thin, the fish leave, drop down the tributaries and re–enter the major parent river. It is at the confluences of the tributaries with the Ganges that most of the catching of the mahseer is done. If the monsoon were to continue longer than we had bargained for then the fish would remain up the tributaries and our entire journey would be in vain (especially as it is almost impossible to catch the fish in the tributaries themselves). We knew that we would have to get on to our chosen junction early and simply stay there until the fish began to run past us, but would we have budgeted for enough time to see success?

Metha himself had seen runs of mahseer drop down tributaries after the spawning was done with. He emphasized that the biggest feral fish returned to the Ganges first, hypersensitive to the dropping water. Smaller fish, probably males, accompany them or even wait at the confluence to fertilize the females a last time there. He had seen flotillas of big fish moving backwards down the river in a dark cloud. Once the big female mahseer hit the Ganges, they stay there some days feeding very hard and this is when they are most vulnerable to bait. Soon, though, they disappear into the great impenetrable Ganges and are lost to anglers again until the next spawning season.

Metha looked at the rods that Paul had brought over for the business.

They were made by Paul's own company and have a test curve of about 3lb and are twelve feet in length. Metha looked excited just to handle them, as tackle like this is impossible to find in India. They are light, delicate, flawless in construction and yet have tremendous power. The large 4,500 GT Shimano Bait Runners complement these rods perfectly. Metha agreed with Paul that 18lb line will be our sensible minimum and how I was to regret before long the 15lb stuff on my own spools. We spent some time looking at and testing swivels, plugs, spinners, hooks and any part of the gear that could offer an escape route to a fleeing mahseer. Both Paul and Metha agreed that plugs and spoons should be big and that the predominant colours should be silver, copper, yellow and green. The hooks that these lures are bought with are useless and have to be stripped off and refitted with the Partridge Paul Boote mahseer trebles – probably some of the strongest freshwater trebles made in the world today.

Both men made it quite clear why the mahseer is such a formidable fighter. It is shaped like a barbel – that is a scaled, hugely finned torpedo. It lives all its life in rivers at the very least the size of the Thames at Richmond but which run with the speed of the River Exe or even the River Awe where it leaves the loch. The bed of the Ganges is festooned with pitfalls. Rocks and rapids are everywhere. A 150-yard run is not abnormal and the fish can take you round a bend of the river and be gone. Recently, a German was actually pulled in and away down the stream, where he drowned.

A mahseer seems never to be beaten and when it should give up it still has reserves of power left in it. Over and over, both men said what I was later to find: that the fight of a mahseer alternates between electrifying runs and periods of doggedness when it is easy to believe that the fish is away and the trebles are into a massive boulder. It is in these periods of quiet that the mahseer rests and gathers steam again, snug behind a rock, its pectorals planting it to the bottom immovably. Finally, of course, there is not a net made big enough to cope with their four, five or even six feet of length. They have to be beached and that is not easy with a do or die creature like the mahseer. It is horrifying to think of the damage that a treble could do if it flew from the fish and into a leg at this very last moment.

Both men admit the efficiency of baits for mahseer. Live baits, dead baits and a bread-like paste all catch a fish which will eat almost anything that it finds in the river. However, both men are quite firm in the belief that lure fishing with plug and spoon is the true way to take mahseer. Metha always fishes deep by casting the lure up river and then letting it sink before working it back in. It is imperative to wade as far out as possible to avoid the shallows and to work only the deeper, quicker water. It is vital to spin slowly with a big lure to entice the fish up several feet towards the surface. Once hooked, the important thing is to get beneath the fish and to try and pull it off balance so that it is fighting the current for its stability. Should a fish get down the rapids, it is important to keep the rods high and with a light tension on the reel lead it gradually and gently back up river. Providing the line is not caught round a rock and providing you do not jerk the fish, the mahseer will follow like a lamb in the true salmon-fishing tradition. Indeed, the whole experience is very much like salmon fishing – letting the current work the spoon gently across river and watching the tip throb. Upon the take, though, the resemblance to salmon fishing ends, for these mahseer would strip and empty the normal salmon reel in seconds. It is Paul who emphasized that the clutch should be set firm enough to set the hooks on the strong take and yet give line at the start of that first run. Once this begins, it is vital to loosen the clutch up and let the fish go whilst the angler gets to the bank where he can be more mobile in the battle. The trick then is to follow the fish up or down river trying to slow it, stop it and finally turn it.

The more the two men talked the more unbelievable the runs of these fish began to seem to me. As I sat in that rain-soaked town the thought of contacting one of these fish became more and more improbable to me. The whole episode seemed more like a dream than real life. Were these fish or dragons from a mythical land?

The afternoon wore on and we had tea with this fisherman while he entertained us with his stories of eagles, vultures, panthers and tigers. Several times out there alone in the wild he had been threatened by big cats that had come as close as ten yards to him before ambling off into the jungle. During these tales, Metha's wife and daughter sat listening to the old man. The cameras by now had stopped whirring and George had put his sound equipment away. We were all enthralled by the atmosphere of calm and love which came from the tight little family. We all realized just how richly the Metha's had lived their lives and how many moments of true worth this old man had now got to look back on in his last years.

More Mahseer Heroes

On the way back to the hotel, through the squalid streets of Dehra Dun we were all quiet on the coach thinking back to our afternoon with

Metha. Our hotel had been decked in lights since our departure earlier in the day and was now a great glowing pyramid of red in the night. A wedding was being celebrated there and there were crowds of excited children in the hallway. There we were met by the manager who carried an invitation for us to a party in one of the rich suburbs of the town. We debated, decided to go and went off to dress as smartly as we could. A fleet of taxis arrived to take us to a fine house on the outskirts of the town where there were parks and tree-lined avenues. Outside the high walls and gates of the dwelling there were still dozens of beggars, hands outstretched, as we moved on into the party. The house was fabulously furnished and all the guests were beautifully dressed, the women showered in jewels. The food was a delight, certainly the best that I had tasted since coming to India and the wines were exquisite. Everywhere we went the conversation was brilliant and entertaining, taking in the state of India, world politics and the arts. It was bewildering to believe that only twenty yards from us, the poor were assembling to sleep the night away on the streets, covered by thin blankets even though the monsoon rain was still pelting down upon them.

I talked to an Indian who had studied philosophy at Oxford. Half a century before he had begun his education at the famous Doon School in Dehra Dun.

'Ah yes, Metha is a hero, no doubt, but he is not alone you know. Let me give you the example of Holsworth, my beloved teacher all those years ago at the Doon School. He was, I think you would say now, a superhero! You know he was known and famous throughout India. (I remembered seeing his photograph held proudly by Mr Goffhara in Kashmir.) There was talk that he was a homosexual. That was the only criticism I ever heard of him and it was absolute rubbish. He was simply a dedicated teacher and his whole life really was lived for the young. Just listen to the man's list of accomplishments. He won a scholarship to Oxford to read three subjects – History, English and Classics. He was a Blue in soccer, hockey and cricket! He even went on to play for Sussex. Upon independence, he tackled dangers in a calm relaxed fashion. As a boy I saw him meet crowds with great bravery and talked them out of using violence. He climbed with Tensing and started trekking at Doon School. He also took us mahseer fishing to the beach opposite Black Rock. When you can see that come proud out of the water then you know that the fish will be running down and the taking times will be about right. That tributary opposite the Black Rock was probably, in his day, the most famous place for mahseer in all of northern India. Everybody made for it if they could.

It was on one of the trips to the Black Rock that Holsworth introduced me to Jim Corbett, you know, the great hunter and writer. Corbett was up there ridding the villages of a man-eating leopard, and if you are here looking for heroes, you need not look a lot further than those two, meeting there on the banks of the Ganges. They were both great in their own way and I know Holsworth admired Corbett for his immense courage. Just imagine, sitting out there all night, alone in the jungle, knowing full well that you are being stalked by one of these enormous, ruthless killers. I think that that meeting rather shook Holsworth for he realized how potentially dangerous our trips could be and thereafter he was always really careful to emphasize the safety angle to us. I don't know how things are up there now but you would do well to be careful yourselves.'

We returned and Peter went straight up to his room but was back down in the main body of the hotel in seconds. Whilst we had been away a burglar had climbed over the veranda into his room and taken all his camera equipment. We spent much of the rest of the night answering the laborious questions of the police force. I lay down at long last not too long before dawn. It was still wet outside and the sound of rain and the visions of Ganges heroes conspired to keep me awake even further.

Waiting for the Black Rock

We left Dehra Dun on a day of sunshine in the coach that was to take us to the Ganges Valley. Three hours later I had my first view of the vast swollen river that dwarfed any other I had seen before. A holy town was situated on its banks, a seething mass of human beings swirling through the templed streets. We left there on a road that climbed continually and narrowed every mile of its ascent. Soon the coach was struggling on hairpin bends with the wheels frequently poised over a gorge hundreds of feet down to the roaring torrents beneath. It was one of the worst journeys of my life and mine was not the only ashen face in the coach that morning. It was a relief when we could drive no further and all our goods were loaded on to the porters and mules waiting to greet us. We had perhaps half a dozen hours of daylight remaining to reach our campsite, way, way beneath the road at the junction of the two rivers. I was soon lost in jungle and now I would have no idea how to find my way back to

Breakfast on the Ganges.

that remote campsite. All I remember is sweltering heat and monkeys continually screeching at us from the dense foliage above and around us. We passed small shrines and occasional Indians sitting by shacks drinking tea watching the party pass in utter amazement.

When we arrived on the beach where the tributary flowed into Mother Ganges an entire village was waiting there to greet us. Scores and scores of brown faces looked at us in awe, amusement and with burning curiosity. Paul pushed through them and walked down to the water's edge studying the rivers before him for several minutes. We did not need telling. We could see for ourselves that the Black Rock was visible only by its tip. The Ganges had at least eight feet to fall before we could expect the mahseer run. Tents were pitched, dinner was cooked and we settled into a routine of work, casual fishing and, above all, prayer for dry weather. Days blurred into each other and set a familiar pattern. I woke most days at five and went straight to the river to study the ever-emerging form of the Black Rock. Then the hours were filled swimming, eating, filming, exploring the valleys and when the sun climbed simply reading in the shelter of the river cliffs as the temperature soared to well over 120°F. Occasional thunderstorms frightened us but the weather remained dry and the river fell slowly but surely. As time grew ever tighter, we began

Not a mahseer but, when times were hard, welcome all the same.

to fish the tributary in the desperate hope of waylaying dropping fish. We walked miles and took risks to reach unfished pools, until one evening I found myself dropping down a scree that I had no hope of ever reclimbing. It was then that I met my shopkeeper.

The tiny village above us had a store about the size of a British bathroom and that night the owner was out on the river. He saw my plight and came down to give me his hand to lead me up the dizzying rock-face back to the track. Our friendship was immediate and his devotion to me over the next fortnight was touching. I awoke each day to find him outside my tent and he would stay hovering like my constant shadow until night fell once more. His shop was shut for the duration as he carried my tackle, stroked my back in affection and laughed uproariously whenever I spoke to him in words that he had no knowledge of whatsoever. He, in his turn, told me jokes about the life of the valley and I understood not a word. Our only mutual words were 'OK' and 'fish'. This did not matter and perhaps it even saved our relationship! We never tired of each other jabbering away in our own tongue and smiling constantly. Right at the end of our stay he undertook the gruelling climb back to the road and the bus just to say farewell to me. My parting gifts to him amounted to a quarter bottle of rum, a couple of spinners and a sun hat and you would have thought that he had just received the crown jewels.

Those first few days saw the valley humid and frequently misty but as the sun grew hotter the colours became more intense and the mountains around more vivid. It was a very, very beautiful place, bejewelled by the most wonderful butterflies, by fabulously coloured birds, by screeching monkeys, by the small shrines so white against the blue of the skies. Those skies remained blue and the Ganges forever dropped.

The village, to an extent, became more used to us. The women were quite willing now to wash openly and merely look up in amusement and interest as we walked past. The men came down to play cards with our porters and to drink small bottles of rum that we gave them out of friendship. The children now liked to play with us rather than run away screaming whenever we talked or approached them. In most ways, the affection that we felt for this little village was warmly repaid and I do believe that if I could ever find my way back I would meet with a warm welcome. Our days passed calmly with few highlights. Once the local barber visited and gave Peter the most manic of crew-cuts and me the bloodiest shave of my life. One night we had a party on the beach with massive bonfires crackling and throwing their sparks to the stars. That was the night Dinesh took up his guitar and sang the most wonderful Nepali love songs that so moved John the Cam that he got hopelessly drunk, pretended to be an aeroplane on the beach and ploughed unconscious into his tent.

6 a.m. on 9 September. John's legs still poked out of the flap of his tent. I wandered past the dying embers to the beach and the Black Rock was standing quite noticeably proud eighty yards out in mid-river. I sensed that things were about to change. Once the rest of the crew were awake we made a trip up the tributary river to a lovely pool, deep in the jungle. In the clear water I saw a mahseer of some 12–15lb follow my plug in before disappearing into a gorge. Paul, too, saw a very large fish coming down through white water. There was an electricity now that Paul and I felt and which communicated itself to all the crew. Lunch was taken under the awning as usual but conversation was rather tight and tense and everyone had mahseer on their minds.

A Tale of Four Days

I quote now from my diary written at 7 p.m. on the evening of 9 September:

'I have just had the most electric two hours fishing of my life. The facts are simple, three fish hooked and lost for me and one fish hooked and landed for Paul: a 26-pounder that was two feet of golden scaled wonderment. I feel absolute elation. The fight was electrifying and the first I had seen of such dogged power and powerful runs. I am really glowing with pleasure for Paul. His head was on the chopping block and now it's saved. We are all saved and the film is on its way. Those lost fish of mine will stay with me for ever. The first was a run of just under 100 yards and I was powerless before it. The hooks were mangled by the teeth of the monster. The thing that I reeled in over the water was hardly recognizable as the plug that I had cast out only a minute before . . . just a mish-mash of crushed wood, plastic and metal. The second mahseer I lost was my own stupid fault. The plug was ripped away from line that was too weak . . . line which broke my heart after only a minute of the contest! The third fish I lost at the end of 150 yard run! The hook-hold simply failed. It was not my fault, just the ill luck that dogged me this afternoon. Still, in total I have been in contact three times with big mahseer and I have had my arms half torn off. I have had five of the most electrifying angling minutes of my life. I asked George what to write and he said, 'Just put down flaming fantastic, mate, flaming fantastic'.

Marvelling mahseer.

That night the crew were as excited as the anglers. It was a dinner of constant jokes over beers and that infamous Indian rum Old Monk. We all began to think of home at last, and now, with a fish on camera, to think of titles for the film that we knew now would be screened. The award of the night went to John the Cam for his 'Dahl M for Mahseer!' I retired at last, not a little drunk, to the tent, still thinking of the next day on the river. Not that I could sleep. Those three mahseer worked continually in my mind, launching through the Ganges at my plugs, all sinew and scale and gold. They had mouths like tunnels and fins like sails. They were savage creatures that were as wild in the waters as the leopards were in the jungles.

The next morning the dream continued. We began fishing a little after five in the morning and by breakfast time we had landed four more mahseer to 30lb. More fish were lost and the whole session seemed to be a mad whirl of screeching reels, juddering rods and the triumphant yell, 'Fish on!' At the end of the morning we had the four fish swimming around the lagoon on ropes, rebuilding their energies, ready to be put back into the main flow of the Ganges. They looked almost as big and as golden as galleons at dock, just finning the water, their great backs exposed to the sunlight.

The next sunset, Paul hooked an enormous mahseer. It was probably the most extraordinary fish I have seen in well over thirty years of angling life. This really was the great golden mahseer that we had come to catch and I feel all of us, whether fishermen or not, rather stood in awe before it. There is no point describing that fish. It would be easy to talk about scales like sovereigns and fins worn down through thousands of miles of river travel, but the atmosphere on the river bank in the dust and the glow of fish really defies words. The feeling that the quest now had been supremely capped swept us all.

12 September.

This had to be the last day on the river and the conditions looked absolutely perfect. In the morning session I landed one fish just over 20lb but lost a much larger one that got me over rapids where I could not follow. The day continued with a tingling suspense and then, in the late afternoon, the last session of this Asian journey began. Dinesh took a rod and landed his biggest ever mahseer of 27lb. Peter too, was quickly in and landed a 42-pounder. Paul and I struggled fishless until, with the most electrifying thump, my own plug was taken. For two minutes I swore that it was simply the bed of the Ganges. There was no movement and

Dawn on the Ganges . . .

. . . and a boy hauls in his night line.

He comes to sell us his catch.

Sun up and we are fishing.

Fish on.

Always, there are anxious moments.

Boote piles on the pressure.

Safe at last.

there was no give and no matter how I pounded on the pressure there was no indication that I was into a living creature. Suddenly that changed and all hell broke loose. I was scrambling over the stones, falling, cursing, cut, soaked, in hopeless pursuit of a flying monster. That fish ran 150 yards downstream before I stopped it or more truly it stopped itself. For a minute it sulked and then it set off up river in a blistering whirlwind charge for quarter of a mile. For most of that fight I was totally out of control and the fish, I always felt, was doing much as it pleased. After virtually an hour, however, things obviously were changing. Now the creature was just five or six yards from me, still very deep, still clamped to the bottom but now I knew for sure that I had him. The shadows were long and the moon was rising when my shopkeeper began to wade out to lift the creature clear. I could see very little but his bent form and a long back slowly, tiredly working against the water in front of him. He made a move to touch the fish and it squirmed out of his grasp. I stopped it comparatively easily and brought the fish back to him. Now I could see the mahseer for myself. It was enormous. Again the shopkeeper bent down and cradled the fish in his arms and for a second time the power of the fish defeated him and it wobbled slowly out towards the main current.

A rope tethers the fish until it recovers . . .

. . . and can be returned to Mother Ganges.

I turned it but only for a second before the plug leapt clear of the cavernous mouth. The fish still lay on its side, gasping. The shopkeeper caught it by the tail. There was a flurry of spray and cursing and a bow-wave moving slowly out and disappearing into the dark water. This last great fish was not to be mine and I sat in despair on the bank.

I had lost a fish that I felt sure was certainly the largest creature that I had ever had on rod and line. That mahseer was the fifth big fish that I had lost and I began to wonder if my trip was in some way cursed. Every angler endures bad runs but this was a trip out of a nightmare. The shopkeeper sat with me whilst the crew and the spectators disappeared back to the camp for their last night of celebrations. He put his arm around me and clucked softly like an adoring mother hen. Then he smacked me on the back sharply and leapt up and down and pointed at the moon that was now riding high and clear. 'Fish. Fish.' He picked up my rod and walked to the water side, made a casting motion and beckoned me to his side. I remembered then what Metha had told me a fortnight before, back in rain soaked Dehra Dun: 'Nights of the full moon often fish better than any day time. If you get the chance try it.'

Peter goes on to hook a 42-pounder!

I checked the hooks of the plug and they were intact. I moved back to that historic spot opposite the Black Rock and began to work down the Ganges as I had done over and over before. Fifth cast and I was into another fish. Playing a big mahseer under the moonlight was like no other experience I had ever had. It was just me and the river at last and this great friend of mine from an alien continent. I could soon tell that the fish was not one of massive weight but its speed and power under those beautiful surroundings healed my heart. This time at the bank my shopkeeper made no mistake and a wonderful fish a full yard long lay glowing under the night sky. This one I gave my friend and he took it back in glory and triumph to feed his family and his neighbours for several days.

There was a lot of talk that night and conversations flowed everywhere. Many were just pleased to be going home and others wished that they could stay on. For myself I was generally quiet, feeling that I had witnessed something of an angling miracle. An idea that had been born in a London office over a year before had finally come to fruition. A dream that I had nurtured as a child a quarter of a century before had now become a reality. The mighty mahseer was no longer a fable for me. I even realized that there was some purpose behind losing that last monster fish. Had I have landed it I could have pretended that my business in Asia was complete but seeing it lost at that very last moment would guarantee that I would have to return. In fact, no sooner had I landed at Heathrow than I was on the phone and writing to contacts, trying to arrange a second trip. Truly, once mahseer are in the bloodstream there is no easy remedy or cure. Metha had said that mahseer are a passion for life and he was right. I had truly undergone four days that had changed my entire consciousness.

To Kill or Not To Kill

The second day of the mahseer run, I think it was Paul who caught a fish, let it recover and returned it lovingly to the river to the accompaniment of what I realized was a stifled groan in the group of a hundred or so Indians behind us. Later on that same night, over the campfire, I talked to Dinesh about the reaction of the village to our western sporting ethics. At first, he refused to be drawn. In his typical, twinkling Nepali way he laughed over the matter, patted me on the shoulder and called for more beers. I pushed him further. I demanded to know and he could see that I was sincere and his mood sobered. 'Remember,' he said, 'these mahseer run only once a year and many years the water is not low enough for these poor villagers to net them. You have had very very big fish and you put them back in front of hungry eyes and rumbling bellies. Any one of those fish would have fed this village for a night and perhaps, you know, have saved a child or two during the hard times that come to all these villages.' 'You want to know how they feel,' he continued, 'for sure, there is resentment. You see sport. They see waste. It is good to be friendly and to play games with the children. Your gifts are appreciated too, but that does not mean they all forgive. The good thing is that we are not killing them and eating them ourselves. At least the mahseer we did eat we bought from the village itself. Those rupees will come in damned useful I tell you.'

I knew myself we were objects of intense interest to the village. Our fishing method fascinated the men and they and the children were agog at the battles they saw filmed on the beach of the great river. Why, we were even the first Europeans many of the younger men and women had seen and both our colour and hairy skin fascinated them. The delicacy and power of the rods, the technical proficiency of our reels and the complexity of our terminal tackle made gods of us to fisherman who spun without rods and whose line was coiled by hand into a tin or on a stout stick.

The end is nigh . . .

The next day we killed a 9lb mahseer and we went up the path to the village to present it. Attitudes thawed. Crowds followed us around the streets into the little temple. Within the village now, it was time to forget the splendour of the mountains and the majesty of the river and just to look at the poverty of our hosts. I caught two mahseer that evening. Both went to the village.

There is nothing wrong with our western coarse fishing ethics. They are essential in the country we live in and I would dearly like to see them spread to the game side of the sport. A single salmon per rod per day ought to be a rule everywhere and surely the big, near-wild browns of Rutland and Grafham should, too, be slipped back. I can say this and yet argue just as strongly that at least a few fish caught in another land of different culture should be killed and taken to the village pot.

The Aftermath

Life after India had its contentments, its hot baths, its plain, predictable food, its cool, its showers, its hygiene and its oozing layers of security. There were also Indian legacies. Within two weeks, I had sprouted the

A mightily finned mahseer.

most foul, festering boils in my armpits and groins, needed fourteen–plus hours sleep a day and found the doctors would not touch me without rubber gloves. More subtly, there was a psychological withdrawal from India to endure. A land that had frequently seemed intolerable and harsh had wormed its way into my mind every bit as much as into my body and I found that before long, I was missing it sorely. There was also the growing feeling that I had not finished my business with the mahseer of the continent entirely either and I did not like to think that the adventure had reached a final act. I knew I would have to return to India and the question of how and when began to haunt me. Unfinished business in the British Isles is quite easily rectified. A return to Asia is much more problematical.

My contract demanded that I travel to London almost weekly through the winter to do and re–do my voice–overs on the film. I disliked the train, detested the tube and was frankly terrified of the studio. I had to squirm through the film rushes and then write a script that sounded even more wooden. I was told in one heated interview that I read with the passion of a parrot!

Eventually came the preview in Granada's London studio. The small cinema, stuffed with the critics of the land, was my own arena of misery. For an hour I sat sweating until the lights came on and a measure of

My dear Joy Cameron as a young mahseer fisherlady.

A fishing film.

applause ended the ordeal. Lunch was a welter of interviews. An intense-eyed lady from a women's magazine said, 'It seems to me that fishing can be compared with childbirth. Do you agree?' I looked blank. My tomato rolled off my slipping plate. 'Look, think of all that physical drama in the fight. Then there is the way you cradle the fish at the end. All this obsession with weight. The care of the fish and its loving return. The whole concept of a creation emerging from the waters with agony and ecstasy. There is a strange cross between ugliness and beauty in both acts. Are you married? No! For you a fish is quite obviously a child substitute! You poor, poor man.'

More dictaphones whirled. 'So mahseer is a sea fish.' 'Could the blow of a mahseer tail break your leg, do you think?' On and on it went, that never-ending, centrally heated, fitted-carpet afternoon that made me long for the wind on my face and the rain in my hair. I escaped into the wet reality of a London side street and concentrated hard on the mountains. Any mountains would do – Scottish, Indian, Irish, anywhere away from this place of alien people.

The film was shown, reviews were favourable and friends were generously kind. For a few weeks I would be stopped in the streets and in bars by interested anglers and would have to tell again for their benefit the

[140]

story of those gigantic fish of the Ganges. In the States, it seemed that the film was even more warmly received and that it won some type of award in Houston. Perhaps best of all was a lovely letter that I received very shortly after the programme was shown. The envelope was post-marked Yorkshire 1989, though in essence it came altogether from another age.

My dear John

You just don't know how happy your programme of last night has made an old widow of seventy-seven. Oh, the memories and the good life I had in India for thirty-six years. I thank you with my heart.

I was born in India in 1912 and my father was a chartered accountant on the railways so I travelled a lot around the Himalayan region. Dehra Dun brings back so many memories as it was the place of my school days and the Ganges was never very far away from every bungalow we lived in.

In those days many Europeans lived in Dehra Dun and we girls would run down to the river's edge and watch the men fishing. Little did I know in all those eleven years at school that I would meet my husband in the army and become mad on fishing myself.

After we were married in 1938, my whole life became an obsession with fishing. Oh those thrills catching the mighty mahseer, the king of fish. It was not in the Ganges that we caught our biggest fish but in a place 120 miles from Rawalpindi where we were posted before the Partition. The finest and largest mahseer had been caught here as this is the place where the River Pooch from Kashmir and the River Ghelum from India meet. There are two bungalows each side of the rivers and we always stayed on the Kashmir side nearer the water. We made weekend trips and sometimes stayed for a whole week at a time. We would sleep under the stars and fish almost all day except in the afternoon when even the mahseer dozed. Near the bungalows was a very deep rock cave and pool and you could look down and see the enormous mahseer hardly moving. What a sight it was and only seeing is truly believing. My late husband's biggest catch was $22\frac{1}{2}$lb but a friend caught one at 48lb. My own largest fish was 21lb and I got this trolling with my favourite Kashmiri gillie. I wish one day that you could make a trip to this same place and I would think of all the anglers who could enjoy the programme you could make.

Forgive me for rambling on but I am afraid it is so long since I have written to someone so interested in Indian fishing that my memories have just come tumbling out. I am very lucky now being looked after in my old age in comfort by my family but your programme brought back to me the most precious and vivid years of my life. I thank you very deeply for that.

My sincere good wishes

Joy Cameron

Other fishing books published by The Crowood Press

Chub and Dance   *John Bailey and Roger Miller*
A comprehensive account of chub and dace angling on the rivers of Great Britain.

Perch: Contemporary Days and Ways   *John Bailey and Roger Miller*
The first major study of perch and perch fishing.

Roach: The Gentle Giants   *John Bailey*
Analyses standard methods and modern developments, and discusses every major British roach venue, both stillwater and river.

Bob Church's Guide to Trout Flies   *Bob Church*
Comments on use and dressing details of 400 of Bob Church's favourite flies (wet, dry, nymphs and lures).

Stillwater Trout Tactics   *Bob Church and Charles Jardine*
Advice from two members of the English Fly Fishing Team about catching trout in stillwaters.

Handbook of Fly Tying   *Peter Gathercole*
A guide, in full colour, to tying a wide range of flies, with every step illustrated with a colour photograph.

Fishing with Bill Sibbons   *Clive Graham-Ranger*
Clive spent a year fishing with Bill Sibbons to produce this account of the man whose ability to take big trout from small waters has become legendary.

The Beach Fisherman's Compendium   *John Holden*
A guide to long-range casting which also covers rods, reels, accessories and rigs.

Quest for Barbel   *Tony Miles and Trefor West*
The most complete handbook on barbel fishing ever produced.

Fly Fishing for Salmon and Sea Trout   *Arthur Oglesby*
The first really comprehensive work to deal almost exclusively with fly fishing techniques.

Tactical Fly Fishing for Trout and Sea Trout on River and Stream *Pat O'Reilly*
An in-depth look at this most mobile form of fishing.

Pike: In Pursuit of *Esox lucius* *Martyn Page and Vic Bellars*
The most complete book on pike fishing, both in Britain and abroad.

Big Carp *Tim Paisley and Friends*
A selection of stories and much advice on how to catch carp over 25lb by many of the top men in the sport.

Trout Angler's Angles *Alan Pearson*
More thoughts, ideas and advice from one of the best known trout fishermen.

To Rise a Trout *John Roberts*
A highly acclaimed handbook giving practical and authoritative advice on dry-fly fishing on rivers and streams.

Trout on a Nymph *John Roberts*
Companion to *To Rise a Trout* which looks at subsurface fishing for trout.

Waddington on Salmon Fishing *Richard Waddington*
The latest thoughts from perhaps the greatest salmon fisherman of the century; full of thought-provoking ideas.

Further information from **The Crowood Press (0672) 20320**.